Trade with China

edited by
Patrick M. Boarman
with the assistance of
Jayson Mugar

Sponsored jointly by
the Center for International Business
Pepperdine University, Los Angeles and Malibu
Richard C. King, Executive Director
and the Graduate School of Business Administration
University of Southern California, Los Angeles
Dr. Ted R. Brannen, Dean

Trade with China
Assessments by Leading Businessmen and Scholars

PRAEGER SPECIAL STUDIES IN INTERNATIONAL ECONOMICS AND DEVELOPMENT

Praeger Publishers　　New York　Washington　London

Library of Congress Cataloging in Publication Data

Boarman, Patrick M   comp.
     Trade with China.

     (Praeger special studies in international economics
and development)
     Papers presented at two conferences sponsored
jointly by the Center for International Business, Pepperdine University and the Graduate School of Business Administration, University of Southern California, June and
Oct. 1972, in Los Angeles.
     Bibliography: p.
     1. United States—Commerce—China—Congresses.
2. China—Commerce—United States—Congresses.
3. China—Economic conditions—Congresses.
I. Title.
HF3120.B6   382'.0973'051   74-1727
ISBN 0-275-28853-6

PRAEGER PUBLISHERS
111 Fourth Avenue, New York, N.Y. 10003, U.S.A.
5, Cromwell Place, London SW7 2JL, England

Published in the United States of America in 1974
by Praeger Publishers, Inc.

Printed in the United States of America

FOREWORD
by Richard C. King
and Dr. Ted R. Brannen

One of the most remarkable aspects of the current great thaw
in the relations between China and the Western world is the precipitate
pace of the process, both before and since President Nixon's historic
visit in February 1972. While the dramatic shift in China's posture
vis-à-vis the West, and especially the United States, clearly opens
up a range of interesting possibilities with respect to both politics
and economics, the speed of the transition has caught many Western
traders, and their opposite numbers in China, somewhat unprepared
to deal effectively with the evolving opportunities and risks inherent
in the new situation.

There are, first, a number of important questions relating to
the global framework of China's relations with the West that urgently
need answers, however provisional.

On the political level, for instance, the opening of a new era of
friendly relations between the United States and the People's Republic
to replace the mutual hostility of the recent past is, on its face, a
positive development for both Americans and Chinese. At the same
time, the direct interest of the People's Republic in having a friendly
United States at its back in its ongoing struggle with the Soviet Union
cannot be ignored, nor can the interest of the United States in having
a well-disposed People's Republic to which it can appeal in its search
for a new and stable multipolar structure of great powers as an in-
strument to achieve permanent peace and order in the world. From
the standpoint of the United States, the political and strategic risks
involved in such an undertaking, especially those having to do with
the real nature of Chinese intentions in the long run, are in essence
no different from those encountered in pursuing détente with the Soviets.
And presumably these risks, including China's continued support of
various revolutionary and guerrilla movements in Asia and uncertainty
about the future policies of the inevitable new leadership in China,
have been and will continue to be set against the immense benefits of
a generation or more of world peace.

Not only the political but also the economic risks and opportunities of doing business with China demand searching scrutiny.
Especially in the realm of trade and investment, the short-term
euphoria emanating from the great thaw should and will be tempered,
on both sides, by objectivity and realism. Many questions need to be
asked. For example, while it seems obvious that the industrialized
countries of the West, especially the United States, have many things

v

the Chinese need and desire, what can they offer us that we need, and on what terms, relative to terms obtainable elsewhere? Can we be sure that the complete technologies and whole plants China is seeking from the West will not one day be used against us, economically and/ or strategically, in some new turn of Chinese ideology? Or is it safe to assume that ever closer economic involvement of China with the West will tend to move the People's Republic further from the doctrinal obsessiveness that produced the Great Leap Forward and the Cultural Revolution? The composition and quantity of U.S.-China business dealings will be decisively affected by how these hazards and opportunities are assessed, both at governmental levels and in the Western business community.

It is answers to these and similar questions that the present compilation of papers on trade with China is intended to supply. The papers are based on two major conferences on trade with China sponsored by the Center for International Business on June 12-13, 1972, at the Los Angeles Hilton Hotel, and by the Graduate School of Business Administration, University of Southern California, on October 9-10, 1972, at the Century Plaza Hotel in Los Angeles. Both institutions were exceptionally fortunate to secure as participants in these meetings businessmen, academicians, and government officials from the United States and other Western countries who are uniquely qualified by their knowledge and practical experience to discuss the subject of trade with China. Their credentials are supplied in the brief biographies that appear at the end of the book.

The conference papers, specially edited for this book, supply a cross section of expert opinion on a range of subjects that are of crucial importance to anyone interested in, or currently engaged in, business dealings with the People's Republic. With the exception of one paper by a government official, the material has not appeared in any form elsewhere. The colloquial flavor of many of the presentations was deliberately retained to make for easier and quicker reading. Material that was essentially transitory or peripheral to the major subjects of discussion was deleted.

Because in China especially, politics is inseparable from economics, Part I examines the political and foreign policy parameters within which the evolution of the West's trade relations with the People's Republic is occurring, and the probable future shape of such relations under various assumptions about the ideological path China chooses and about its attitudes toward other great powers.

Both the opportunities and the limits of China's ability to engage meaningfully in international trade are set by its resource base and the internal requirements arising from that base, by its ability to generate exportable surpluses of goods and services, by its foreign exchange reserves, by the way in which China's centrally planned economy operates, and by the interplay within China between its major political and economic goals. These matters are the subject of Part II.

Taiwan (the Republic of China) is a thriving economic entity whose domestic and foreign economic successes somewhat resemble, on a smaller scale, those of Japan. The severance of diplomatic relations with Taiwan by more than 30 countries that have established formal relations with Peking has not noticeably affected the internal politics or economics of Taiwan. Led by a boom in Taiwan's exports of light manufactured goods, the economy has attained growth rates that surpass even the remarkable performance of the 1960s. Japanese and Western businessmen, especially Americans, continue to have a substantial stake in Taiwan's economic future, both in terms of investments already there and in terms of the burgeoning opportunities for future investment and trade. The largest single investment ever made in Taiwan by an American corporation—$36 million by the Ford Motor Company to buy control of a local automobile manufacturer—was approved in the autumn of 1972. General Motors is currently assessing the possibility of joining in a similar deal with another Taiwan company. Part III explores the exceedingly important question of how Taiwan fits into the overall pattern of U.S.-China relations and considers some of the areas of conflict that are likely to arise for those who want to do business with both Taiwan and Peking.

Parts IV and V contain evaluations of the short-term and long-term opportunities for trading with China by persons with extended firsthand experience in the China trade and pragmatic assessments of the administrative and legal hurdles—on both sides—that will have to be overcome if the existing trade potential is to be exploited effectively. Some of the questions raised include the following: Will China eventually agree to accept long-term credits from Western countries and Japan, the current rejection of which sets obvious limits on China's ability to pay for imports? What kinds of goods and services is China most likely to purchase from other countries? What does China have in the way of exports, or of export potential of interest to Western buyers? What are the formalities, administrative and legal, that need to be gone through in order to establish effective contact with Chinese buyers and Chinese sellers on world markets?

Part VII is a case study of American business operations in China as recounted by the president of RCA Global Communications (the foreign operations division of RCA). It was RCA that put in place, for permanent Chinese use, the internal and external communications network that made possible the comprehensive television coverage of President Nixon's visit.

Part VIII consists of 20 statistical tables on various aspects of China's involvement in the international economy. Part IX is a bibliography, intended primarily for English-speaking businessmen, of recent articles, books, and other materials dealing with the economics and politics of both Taiwan and Mainland China.

Trade with China is a joint venture of the Center for International Business and the Graduate School of Business Administration of the University of Southern California. Special tribute is due in this regard to Dean Alan J. Rowe of the Graduate School of Business Administration of USC for his efforts in arranging for the collaboration between the two institutions. We believe the present book makes an extremely valuable contribution to public understanding of China's new role in the world economic community and of its economic relations with the United States in particular. It is also, as noted, a pragmatic guide for businessmen and government officials through the complexities—psychological, economic, legal, and political—that surround such relations. The stakes of both the United States and China in a successful further development of economic intercourse between them may be presumed to be large; but only patient attention to the laying of the foundations, including prudent regard to the political and economic realities that both must face, assures such a development. That is the major purpose of this book.

> Richard C. King, Executive Director
> Center for International Business
> Pepperdine University
> Dr. Ted R. Brannen, Dean
> Graduate School of Business Administration
> University of Southern California

> Los Angeles
> Spring 1974

Many of the papers in this book project sizable increases in U.S.-China trade. But the actual magnitude of the increase in such trade as reflected in the latest available figures exceeds even the most optimistic forecast made as the material was being edited for publication. Two-way U.S.-China trade for 1973 totalled about $800 million and is expected to amount to $1.2 billion for 1974, which would represent a tenfold increase over 1972. Admittedly, this spectacular growth proceeded from a very low base, but the reality of the change in the absolute level of trade is impressive enough.

The key question is whether such trade may not be rapidly approaching some sort of upper limit in virtue of China's ability to pay for further purchases from the United States. U.S. imports from China were only $65 million in 1973 as against over $700 million of U. S. exports to China. While U.S. imports are expected to rise to over $100 million in 1974, with exports projected at more than $1 billion this still leaves a huge imbalance in favor of the United States. It is true that some offset is available from Chinese surpluses with third countries disposing of convertible currencies, but these are not presumed at present to be increasing rapidly enough to finance ever larger deficits with the United States. Thus, the further expansion of U.S.-China trade will be determined primarily by the possibility of significiantly increasing U.S. imports from China or, alternatively, by China's abandonment of its hitherto rigid refusal to accept long-term foreign funding of its trade deficits (a question which is touched upon in several of the papers that follow).

The fundamental constraint on the trade side—and this is similar to that which burdens the U.S.-USSR trade relationship—is that China's traditional exportables are quite limited in quantity and quality and what is available appears to have low potential salability in the U.S. market.

One exit from the trade-imbalance dilemma may lie in a greatly expanded exploitation of China's raw material reserves, especially petroleum. Intense efforts are underway now to expand production in the vast Taching field in northern China, first opened at the beginning of the 1960s. In fact, Taching is proving to be a huge bonanza with almost no end in sight to the reserves. The pace of its development is limited only by an unsufficiency of modern drilling equipment. Oil from the Taching pool is already being exported, though as yet in modest quantities, to Japan (one million tons annually), to Hong Kong, and to the Philippines. Expanded surveying of China's offshore oil is also underway and, in tandem with the activity at Taching and other established fields, has produced a spate of Chinese orders for sophisticated drilling equipment and for refinery and petrochemical technology from the West, including a recent multimillion dollar order placed with a California manufacturer.

Whether the Chinese will assent to the export of their oil in quantities sufficient to overcome the trade imblance and whether they will do so at prices that are acceptable to the United States are questions to which only the future can supply answers.

It is precisely here that the newest wave of cultural and political turbulence in China has cast a shadow not visible when the present papers were in preparation. While the current campaign against Confucius, Lin Piao, Beethoven, Schubert, and the Italian film producer Antonioni does not appear to be even approaching the convulsive fury of the Cultural Revolution of 1965-69, the bloom is definitely off the rose of U.S.-China cordiality planted in the wake of the Nixon visit of 1972. Anti-American rhetoric is being heard more often, the number of visas granted to American visitors to China has dropped noticeably, and the head of the Chinese liaison office in the United Staes has yet to return to his post following his departure in the winter of 1973. If the improvement of U.S.-China relations was initiated, as some argue, mainly as a Chinese tactic to counter the U.S.-Soviet detente, the cooling of that detente in recent months may also have reduced the Chinese interest in a further movement toward "normalization." Otherwise, what is one to make of Premier Chou's ridicule, in the spring of 1974, of promises of "a generation of peace"—the celebrated phrase of his erstwhile guest, President Nixon—and his observation that "so long as imperialism exists, revolution and war are inevitable"?

What needs to be remembered, as Barry Richman notes in a paper included in this book, is that ". . .[Chinese] development has been and will continued to be ideological. . .a decision to let the economy even fall apart for ideological reasons and, in the process, to ignore growth and efficiency, and so on, is based on a trade-off calculation between how fast they want social change and the development of a new type of Communist man, and how fast they want the economy to go."

Added to these uncertainties is, of course, the question of who will lead China as age and death remove Mao and Chou from the scene: the hardliners, fearful of contamination by imperailists, or the liberals, determined to end China's xenophobic isolation from the world?

The economic and ideological "ifs" that currently encompass U.S.-China relations do not now seem weighty enough to dissuade China's planners from continuing on the path on which they have embarked of acquiring as much Western, and especially American, technology and resources as they can. Likewise, American and other Western businessmen continue to be fascinated by the possibilities of doing business, more business, with a nation of 800 million people. On the assumption that this mutuality of interests prevails, the analyses offered hereinafter have abiding relevance and importance.

Patrick M. Boarman
Los Angeles
Summer 1974

SPONSORS' ACKNOWLEDGMENTS

The sponsors of the original conferences, and of the present publication, wish to thank all those who helped to make possible this unique manual on China trade:

—the conference speakers, who spent considerable time and trouble in revising and updating their papers for this book;

—Dr. Patrick M. Boarman, director of research of the Center for International Business, for his signal editorial achievement in reducing a vast mass of taped material from the conferences to a coherent and readable manuscript, as well as for the valuable bibliography of recent literature dealing with the trade, politics, and economics of Taiwan and Mainland China prepared under his direction;

—Jayson Mugar, international economist with the Union Bank of Los Angeles and a member of the student body of the Graduate School of Business Administration, University of Southern California, who ably assisted Dr. Boarman in the initial editing of the manuscript and who also played a major role in organizing USC's China trade symposium;

—Doyle Swain, director of special projects at the Center for International Business, who bore the primary responsibility for the organization of the Center's China trade meeting;

—Patty Terhune, the Center's able secretary, who assumed the brunt of the typing burden; and Bernhard Hess and Gregory Rossoff for their painstaking efforts in helping to produce the final version of the book.

CONTENTS

THE POLITICAL
AND FOREIGN POLICY
FRAMEWORK

1

THE PEOPLE'S REPUBLIC OF CHINA: POLITICAL TRENDS AND FOREIGN RELATIONS
by David Wilson

It is now over two years since President Nixon went to China and made his remarks about the week that would change the world. I think one can forgive his obvious hyperbole. Clearly, the week didn't change the world; but it did change much of the way in which we look at China, and I have been particularly struck by this since I have been in the United States. It has enabled us to slough off a great deal of the previous, rather sterile discussion that we used to have on China; the sort of thing that revolved around the question of whether America should or should not recognize the existence of China. This kind of issue was essentially rather minor, but it enabled people to avoid the larger issues of what China stands for and what Chinese policy is all about. Since President Nixon has been to China, and particularly since the extraordinary press and television coverage of that visit, we can step back a little and take a different sort of look at China, realizing that something fundamental in the relationship between the United States and China has changed but that we are only at the beginning of this new era; we are not at the end of it.

On the other hand, I think that President Nixon's visit has made certain things rather harder. I was reminded of this when I walked in the streets of Los Angeles trying to discover where north was by looking at the stars; you can't see the stars because of all the street lights. To me, the Nixon visit was rather like that. It was like a close-up photo of China that has obscured the rather more important things that are far away. Therefore, I would like to discuss a few of what I consider to be fundamental points of Chinese foreign policy

---

Editor of <u>China Quarterly</u>, Contemporary China Institute, University of London.

and some of the trends that, it seems to me, are apparent in China at the moment.

Essentially, three lines of thought run through Chinese foreign policy and have continued to run through it since the victory of the Communist Party in 1949. The first is the question of the national security and the territorial integrity of China. That has been and remains the fundamental feature of Chinese foreign policy—as, indeed, it would be the fundamental feature of the foreign policy of any new government taking over the situation that existed in China in 1949. If we consider the important developments of Chinese foreign policy since 1950—the war in Korea, the conquest of Tibet, the battle with the Indians on the Sino-Indian border, even President Nixon's visit—this thread is visible. One has to recognize the fundamental importance of the national security of China, which tends to be paramount in times of crisis.

This Chinese concern with territorial integrity has been highly defensive in nature. China has been ringed by powers that had greater strength. She continues to be partly encircled by the Soviet Union, even though her other former antagonist, the United States, is steadily withdrawing from East Asia. Consequently, China has in one sense been forced into a defensive posture. Such a posture, however, has also been the chosen policy of the Chinese government, partly from necessity, partly from preference.

The second of the two characteristics of Chinese foreign policy, and one that is far less easy to define in specific terms, is the search for a return to China's rightful position in the world. China's history over the last 100 or 150 years—as seen by the Chinese, as repeated in all Chinese history books, as repeated in all the schools—is the humiliation of China by foreign powers (of which Britain, of course, was the chief one in the 19th century). This has become a very important psychological aspect of the way in which Chinese government leaders, as well as people lower in the ranks of society, view China's relations with the outside world. It is a factor that long predates the Communist victory in 1949. After all, before World War II, May 7 was set aside as National Humiliation Day, because that was the day on which the Japanese government made certain fundamental and destructive demands on China during World War I.

The idea of China as having been a humiliated state and then rising as a phoenix from the ashes has acquired great importance. It is far from being a vague concept that one might treat as a subject for mild academic debate; it is a concept that affects the way in which Chinese officials deal with people in the outside world. It affects even the handling of China's diplomatic relations. It also affects the way in which China will deal with foreign businessmen (including Americans) when they go to China; and if one doesn't have the sense of this almost self-imposed feeling of humiliation, coupled with the strong belief that China has now risen above this historical humiliation, one can misunderstand the way in which one is treated as a foreigner. Sometimes, it might be added, the way in which one is treated is not very pleasant.

The third fundamental characteristic of Chinese foreign policy is that the leadership of China, both the government and the Communist Party, does have a very different outlook on the world, on the balance of forces in the world, and on what forces should be supported than does the American government or the government of any country in Western Europe. They have both a belief that change will be in their favor (they are not a status quo power) and a belief, stemming from their own ideology, that it is necessary to support certain "progressive forces"—forces struggling for liberation from an old capitalist system—throughout the world. The extent to which this support is given and the manner in which it is given change from year to year, depending on the current policy of the Chinese government. It is a sort of support and commitment that is very often misunderstood when one talks simply of Chinese subversion or Chinese expansion. But to neglect the Chinese belief in the necessity to support what they see as "progressive forces" would be to neglect an important feature of Chinese policy, one that makes the rapprochement between China and a country like the United States a very difficult and, in my view, rather slow process.

These are some of the underlying features of Chinese foreign policy or, perhaps more precisely, of the way in which China looks at the world and in which her foreign policy has worked out. But it is also important to remember that there has been no such thing as a consistent Chinese foreign policy in the years since 1949. It is a very strange thing about foreign policies and the way in which people interpret them that your own country's foreign policy—and the nearer you get to the heart of government, the more this seems true—is generally seen as a series of ad hoc reactions to crises. It goes bumbling along. It is a fudged business in which the administrators try to do their best to meet the crisis that landed on their desks that morning. The policy of any other government, in marked contrast, is seen as being consistent, logical, and perhaps—depending on how you feel about that other country—Machiavellian. It is in this sense easier to see the consistencies in other people's policies than in your own. As far as China is concerned, it is important to realize that the actual manner in which China has operated since 1950 has changed dramatically from period to period, and that there has not been a consistent thread of policy, as opposed to attitude, running through those years.

Although the way in which China looks at the world has generally remained consistent since the late 1960s, the world scene that faces China has changed in a number of important respects. I would like to review briefly these changes that have been external to China, partly to refresh our memories and partly to put them into the proper context. The first change has been the accelerating deterioration of relationships between China and the Soviet Union. Although this deterioration has been going on since the late 1950s, it reached a dramatic point in 1968 and early in 1969 with the clashes on the Sino-Soviet border. It has remained a very large problem for China ever since. After all, the Soviet Union is a very powerful nation and has been continuously moving large forces to its border with China. It is still doing so. China has had to respond by redeploying forces away from the coast opposite Taiwan and up to the northern border. The potential for a real and serious conflict resulting from these relatively minor border clashes in 1969 was, I am convinced, a most serious problem for China's leaders and was one of the factors contributing to the way in which the Cultural Revolution changed at that time, becoming more conservative, and to the restructuring of China's foreign policy that followed.

It might be asked, in connection with China's preoccupation with defense, whether she really could have felt threatened by Tibet, India, or even the Soviet Union. Of course China did not feel threatened by Tibet. The question in the case of Tibet was not one of security for China but of the territorial integrity of China, of putting the boundaries of China back where they ought to have been before they were eroded because of the Revolution of 1911 and its aftermath. The question of Tibet must, however, be distinguished from that of India and the Soviet Union. The Chinese felt that their territorial integrity really was threatened by the Indians. Although this is a complex issue, with much emotion on both sides, it is reasonable to suggest that just prior to the border war, the Indians were assuming a threatening posture. Neville Maxwell's book, India's China War, provides an extremely detailed investigation of that conflict. It is more or less sympathetic to China; I disagree with some of the material but am in agreement with most of it.

In the case of the Soviet Union, China definitely felt her national security to be threatened. It is always a bit of a puzzle to try to distinguish between the reality of what might have occurred and what people believe might have occurred. I think it is reasonable to say that the Soviet Union was not going to attack China. The disadvantages of doing so were enormous, and certainly all the Russians to whom one spoke during that summer of 1969 denied that there was any such possibility. But I believe it is also reasonable to assume that the Chinese leadership thought that there was a fairly good chance that the Russians were going to attack. The Russians threatened by radio, and doubtless by other means, to take out China's nuclear installation and to support subversion in Sinkiang (which has been going on anyhow). An additional factor was that the Chinese felt threatened by the political repercussions in China had there been some sort of military attack that they could not contain. And if the Russians had taken out China's nuclear installations, there was nothing the Chinese could have done about it. It would have been a psychological blow to the Chinese leadership of enormous proportions. Given that there was considerable political confusion in China resulting from the Cultural Revolution, I do not think the Chinese leadership would have been wrong to assume that loss of the nuclear installations might well have led to a major political upheaval. Therefore they had to defuse that situation very rapidly, and they moved to do so in October 1969.

The other major factor that has changed significantly in the past few years, perhaps more in terms of China's perception of it than in reality, is Japan. We should, perhaps, not be too critical of the Chinese for failing to notice, years ago, that Japan was developing rapidly as an economic and (potentially) political power. It is certainly true that in Britain, and to some extent in the United States, many people failed to see the implications of what was happening in Japan. Indeed, it might be argued, parenthetically, that the way in which the visit of President Nixon to China was arranged—without regard to the feelings of Japan—suggested that the United States did not realize the key importance of Japan and what was going on there.

So far as China is concerned, however, it was becoming very apparent by late 1969 that Japan was going to be either the most important factor, or one of the most important, in foreign politics in the next two decades. If one wants to pick a single point in time that brought this home to China, it might be the visit of Prime Minister Sato to the United States in November 1969 and the joint communiqué then signed by him and President Nixon that said, among other things, that Taiwan was considered an area of vital importance to the security of Japan. It is a statement that the Japanese government is now trying to play down. It worried the Chinese very much and brought home to them in a forcible fashion the fact that Japan's economic power and the way in which that power was going to be used politically would be a prime determinant of the evolution of Asia in the next two decades.

One must also take into account the fact that U.S. policy has changed markedly over the past few years, particularly in relation to China. Certain of the obstacles to an improvement of relationships with Peking (such as trade and travel barriers) have been removed with great skill. (I do, however, have some personal reservations about the necessity for President Nixon himself to go to China.) It would be wrong to underrate the effect of the skillful easing of relations

7

on the way in which China has been able to change her own policy. However, it has not been just a question of China's waiting for the United States to behave in a "correct" manner toward China; clearly, there has also been a realization that the United States is at the moment in a weak position in Asia and that China can gain advantage from this. This year may indeed have been the optimum moment for China to gain vital concessions from the U.S. government.

The last way in which the scene has changed recently for the Chinese leadership is the structure of the Chinese leadership itself. This is a factor of considerable importance. The Chinese leadership is, after all, old. This might not matter if there were a successor generation about to appear. But not only is there not an apparent successor generation, there is, more importantly, a realization among the Chinese leadership that the present group of people, particularly Chairman Mao, has an authority within China that a successor generation would not have. In other words, there are certain things that Mao can do, or that can be done when Mao is there, that could not be done when the present leadership and Mao himself are gone. An accepted or legitimate revolutionary leadership is crucial for China. It follows that certain things must be done while the present leadership is still in power.

Connected with both the question of the Chinese leadership and the question of a change in U.S. policy is the problem of Taiwan, America's relations with Taiwan, and the relations of Peking with Taiwan. It seems to me that the time is coming when, if American support for Taiwan, at least in psychological terms, is not withdrawn, the pressures of history and of economics will move in the direction of some form of independence. It is, moreover, probable that this form of independence might well be closely connected in economic terms with Japan. Hence, if this outcome seemed probable, the Peking leadership would consider it worthwhile to seize the opportunity, when America is in a weak position, to try to undermine, psychologically, support for Taiwan and for the Nationalist government.

We have all been impressed by the nature of the change that has taken place in American policy toward China. However, as a result we tend to underestimate the difficulties experienced by China in making her own change of policy—which is as dramatic for China, and possibly more so, than it has been for the United States. The country which has been condemned publicly in China since 1950 as the leading imperialistic nation and the man—President Nixon—who has been personally referred to in fairly vituperative terms, both appeared, as it were, in Peking for a more or less official visit. This was quite difficult to accept, not only for the masses of the Chinese people but also for the elite group composed of members of the Communist Party and government bureaucrats. The opinion of the elite matters in China; and if we consider China to be a country in which the leadership says something and everybody does it, and in which there is no form of public opinion, we are in danger of misinterpreting the way in which things happen in China. I believe that it has been difficult to persuade this elite group to accept the recent dramatic changes of Chinese policy.

There were great disruptions in the leadership in Peking in the summer and autumn of 1971, with the disgrace of the minister of defense, Lin Piao, and a number of very senior military leaders. We do not know that this was necessarily connected with the change of policy toward the United States, but I believe that there was a partial connection. More important, we know from reading the Chinese press that there was a great problem of explaining to the Chinese people the necessity of changing policy toward the United States. When President Nixon left Shanghai, to which point Chou En-lai had accompanied him, Chou flew back to Peking, to an enormous reception at the Peking airport. Much of the press commented that this showed how pleased the Chinese government and Communist Party leadership were with the results of the Nixon visit, and that the mass reception was designed to demonstrate the pleasure with those results. As a cynic who has been trying to look at Chinese affairs for some time, I had a different interpretation: There was great uncertainty among the Chinese leadership about the visit and what might be achieved from it; therefore it was necessary to have a large demonstration of unity at Peking airport for Chou En-lai to show the elite that the people, the government, and the Communist Party were united behind the policy. To me, consequently, it was a demonstration that many people had not been united behind the idea of the Nixon visit.

This point brings one back again to the question of the present leadership in China and what can be done with it that might not be possible later. To revert to the Nixon visit, the first day, after a rather depressing cavalcade through the streets of Peking and the big, empty T'ien An Men Square with nobody watching, there was an unexpected visit by President Nixon to Chairman Mao. The following day the visit was splashed in the People's Daily, the main Peking paper, and on Peking television. The American television people, who were commenting on pictures of the Chinese in Peking queuing up in the main streets to see copies of the People's Daily with pictures of Chairman Mao and President Nixon, remarked that the Chinese people were interested in seeing what the president of the United States really looked like. That, I think, was the wrong interpretation. What the Chinese people were desperately anxious to know was how the visit was being portrayed and what sort of line the government was taking toward it. The fact that Mao met Nixon on the first day and the fact that the People's Daily carried on its front page an enormous picture of the two of them relaxing in Mao's study did give a very significant line. It showed that Chairman Mao had given his personal approval to this dramatic change of Chinese policy. That, to me, suggests that such changes can be made when the people can be shown that the change is an accepted and acceptable policy because Chairman Mao himself has backed it with his personal authority.

That brings me to the question of the trends in China that will affect the future development of relations between the United States and China, including the question of trade. It seems to me that the economy is doing well in China; that it has been doing well in recent years; and that basically, at the commune level, the production of food grains has been doing well for a considerably longer period. Therefore, without going into details, there does seem to be an important stability in the economy. This is reflected also in the official mood in China at the moment. I would like to distinguish between what I call the official mood and a broader mood.

Illustrative of the trend I refer to is a letter I received from an old friend in Peking, a foreigner, for whose opinion on Chinese affairs I have an enormous respect. He wrote that while visiting Peking recently (he has been there many times since 1949), he was very impressed by the fact that Chinese officials, particularly in the Foreign Ministry and Foreign Trade Ministry, were extremely relaxed and self-confident; that they seemed to have a very clear conception of what China was trying to do in terms of foreign policy; but that this self-confidence among the officials was not yet reflected more widely. I know that, in saying this, I am going in diametrical opposition to a number of the comments that have come from American visitors to China in the last few years. I would only beg indulgence and say that I think there is a great difference in impressions of those who have visited China before 1949 and not again until the 1970s (one is bound to be struck by the contrast between what was virtually a civil war and a time of peace) and those who have visited China continuously since 1949 (one tends to see the many negative changes that have resulted from dramatic upheavals in the politics of China, such as the Cultural Revolution). I would, therefore, accept the view that outside the small official groups who deal with foreigners, there is still a great deal of uncertainty among the Chinese population as a result of the Cultural Revolution. This is slowly being cleared away and will diminish as the internal political and economic situation stabilizes. But it would be wrong to assume that such a very large-scale upheaval as the Cultural Revolution can just disappear overnight and leave no effect at all on the minds of the people.

Another great issue (and I revert to it because I think it is so important) is the question of leadership and of succession. In my view, the Cultural Revolution was designed in part to deal with the question of succession and to try to bring new blood into the leadership as well as new attitudes into the way people handled governmental problems. To a very large extent this has been a failure. New blood has not been brought into the top level of leadership except in one or two cases. On the contrary, the leadership has been thinned out, and we are beginning to see what is bound to be one of the trends of the next couple of years: funeral celebrations in Peking for those leaders of the Revolution who have dominated Communist Party affairs and government ever since the 1930s. Chen Yi, the foreign minister, is dead. Hsieh Fu-chih, who was the minister of public security, is also dead. A number of important, but less prominent people also have died.

In short, the group that led the Chinese Revolution and the Communist Party to victory, a group of remarkable ability, is going; and, so far as we can tell, there is not yet a younger group of the same abilities. Indeed, it would be difficult for anybody to match that group, brought up in a period of war and revolution. The successor generation is a problem for any revolution, and I see no reason why China will not encounter it.

I do not want to suggest that a strong regime cannot survive the death of its leaders, but only that a second-generation leadership in any revolution is almost always inferior to that of the first generation. The sort of fuller's fire that creates the first generation doesn't exist for the second. The present leadership has tried to create an ersatz fuller's fire, an artificial revolutionary experience, in order to produce a new generation of leaders.

The Cultural Revolution is obviously a very complex phenomenon, but one of its aspects was this contrived experience of an ersatz revolution, which, it was hoped, would yield new leaders. There would be a clearing away of dead wood and a bringing in of new people. The dead wood was cleared out. What did not happen was the emergence of new people—or, to be more precise, the new people were brought in and then they too, were cleared out. There was a period in 1967 when a number of younger people were brought into fairly senior positions. But they, too, fell into disgrace, accused of extreme leftism, leaving a residual leadership that is very small indeed. The Standing Committee of the Politburo now consists effectively of Chairman Mao, who is 81, and Prime Minister Chou En-lai, who is 75.

If we relate all this to China's foreign policy and its dealings with the outside world, we must consider how these problems will be dealt with over the next few years. We must take into account the fact that in the past, when there have been periods of confusion such as the Cultural Revolution or the Great Leap Forward, the concentration of China's leadership has been turned toward domestic problems. In times of acute crisis, like the Cultural Revolution in

1967 and 1968, foreign relations have been allowed to go by the board. China has simply ceased to have any sort of meaningful foreign policy. Relations in a formal sense may have continued, but there has been no policy. Now, if that has been true in the past, and if it is also true (and I say this with all reservations, because it is a subject on which we don't know enough) that there is not yet a successor generation or organization, and if the present leadership does disappear over the next few years or so, then we must be prepared to see another period in which the internal problems of China will predominate over foreign relations.

I do not mean to suggest that there are necessarily going to be enormous upheavals or civil wars. I don't even mean to suggest that we may hear what is happening among the leadership immediately after the present leaders die; but I would suggest that it is quite possible that there will have to be a great deal of sorting out in Peking and that, during that sorting-out period, we may well see foreign relations take second place.

I would like to sum up by suggesting that there are certain ways in which we should look at China, particularly if we are going to deal with China directly. We need here to distinguish again between two levels. There is a low level of China (without implying any pejorative meaning) that, in the communes and in the factories, is relatively unaffected by what happens in the top leadership. During the Cultural Revolution it was possible for most of the country to be almost unaffected by what was happening in the major cities—Peking, Shanghai, and Canton. Admittedly this was not the case in the factories, but it was true for the countryside. At that level China has made enormous strides since 1950, partly as a result of a period of peace and partly as a result of having a group of very dedicated leaders within the Communist Party and the government. This sort of progress is likely to continue, although at a relatively slow rate. However, this is not the level that is of immediate interest in terms of how we deal with the Chinese. The key people are those one encounters in diplomacy or trade. With respect to this group—the elite, as it were—one must consider its extreme sensitivity to the political atmosphere and to changes in Peking. This is not a matter of everybody jumping to respond to directives from Chairman Mao. It is one, rather, of people who have developed enormously sensitive political antennae and who can respond to what are very far from being direct orders.

As a very minor illustrative digression, if one thinks back to the crisis in Hong Kong in 1967—which was one of very great difficulty for the Hong Kong government—one saw this sensitivity working outside China. A group in Hong Kong was responding to an attitude that they could see in Peking, an attitude of revolutionary ferment and fervor. They were not responding to direct orders from Peking or

Canton that said "Overthrow the British colonial regime in Hong Kong."
Far from it. They were getting no orders, but they were responding
to an atmosphere.

Within China this elite group is even more sensitive. It follows,
therefore, that if one is going to deal with these people in terms of
diplomacy or trade, one must be very closely in touch with the things
that affect them. One must be sensitive to the political changes within
China. One must know what things are important in any given period,
because one will come across them in all discussions, no matter what
the official subject. Certain subjects will be extremely difficult to
handle. Certain subjects will become easier because the mood in
Peking has changed. All this makes dealing with China a matter of
some complexity. It requires enormous patience and a great deal of
reading of material that is not to be found in the daily papers to get
the feeling for the way in which internal politics is developing in China.
Yet it has to be done, and this would be as true if the Kuomintang had
won the civil war in China.

There are great gaps between China and ourselves in respect
to history, culture, and language—in terms not only of translation but
also of concepts that don't translate well. All these have to be overcome before one can have the requisite sensitivity toward China. It
is no easy task.

I was fascinated to discover that China realizes that the reverse
of this problem also exists. To illustrate this point, let me quote
from a recent issue of the theoretical Communist Party journal, Red
Flag, which contains a passage about the necessity to study the history
of foreign countries. It might serve as a leitmotif for our discussions:

> Some comrades feel that it is not easy to remember the
> names of foreigners and foreign places. This is a prob-
> lem frequently encountered by those comrades who
> neglect the study of the history of foreign countries.
> However, if they bear in mind the requirements of cur-
> rent revolutionary struggle and study what is definitely
> the purpose in mind, this difficulty in study can be easily
> overcome. If we study diligently and come into frequent
> contact with them, the names of unfamiliar people and
> places will naturally become familiar.
>   The important thing is that we must be conscien-
> tious. If we are conscientious and perservering, our
> study will certainly be fruitful.

I hope that our endeavors will be fruitful.

CHAPTER

2

U.S.-CHINA RELATIONS
IN THE WAKE OF
PRESIDENT NIXON'S VISIT
by Marshall Green

For more years than I care to count, I have looked to the day
when China trade would be not just a subject of academic interest but
a practical concern of practical men. I would therefore like to place
trade in the framework of our overall relationship with the People's
Republic of China and to suggest why trade figures so importantly in
the momentous changes we are witnessing.

To find a reference point, I could go back a decade or more to
a time when a number of us in the American Foreign Service, together with some of our colleagues in business and academe, were
recommending that tight U.S. restrictions on trade and travel to the
People's Republic be modified and that we enter into a real dialogue
with Peking. Or I could discuss the number of steps that were taken
between 1962 and 1971 in modifying those restrictions, especially the
rapid succession of measures undertaken by the Nixon administration,
from 1969 to 1971, to enable Americans to visit the People's Republic
and to engage in trade. These were unilateral administrative measures
that required no U.S. legislative action or reciprocity from the Chinese
side, and until recently they did not seem to produce much in the way
of results. What changed the whole scene, of course, was President
Nixon's trip to China.

But rather than go over these events that are so well known, I
would prefer to start with the joint communiqué issued at Shanghai
on February 28, 1972. Those who have studied or had some experience
in foreign affairs are well aware that communiqués are often the least
interesting or important results of diplomatic meetings. If that is

---

U.S. ambassador to Australia, formerly (to March 1973) assistant
secretary of state for East Asian and Pacific affairs.

the rule, then the joint communiqué is the exception. It is a remarkable document for several reasons. First of all, it is comprehensive, reflecting all the understandings reached and all the discussions held. It is realistic, making no effort, through either omission or obscure language, to gloss over or minimize the differences that remain between the two nations. On the contrary, it hits them head-on. Indeed, the first area of common ground we found with the Chinese was that this is the style in which we both like to do business. The Chinese, no less than we, do not like to pretend that there are no differences when differences clearly exist.

Having stated our differences, however, we were able to outline possible areas of common interest and to specify ways in which we might work together toward the normalization of relations. Clearly implied in this document was the real breakthrough: that we could move forward without first resolving all those differences. Also clearly implied was the realization on both sides that whatever the broad ideological concerns that divide us, there should be few fundamental differences in practical, national-interest terms that time and mutual trust could not resolve. And, most important of all, we agreed that improving relations was in the interest of both sides.

The communiqué also sets forth the specifics of how we will work to strengthen our relationships. We agreed to maintain contact through various channels, including the sending of a senior U.S. official to Peking from time to time.* Later we announced that another channel or contact point had been established in Paris, where discussions are continuing in the same constructive atmosphere that marked the summit meetings in Peking. We also agreed that increasing contact between our peoples was at least as important as official contact in developing and deepening this new relationship.

Neither of us meant by this that if we just get to know each other better, all our problems will disappear. There was a more practical consideration. For differing reasons, both the People's Republic and the United States evidently want to provide tangible evidence of a warming trend in our relations. Because obstacles to improved relations remain, the communiqué stressed that for the time being, areas of common interest must be sought in less politically charged fields: trade and cultural exchanges.

On the subject of trade, the joint communiqué said:

---

*In early 1973 the United States and China established permanent liaison offices at a high level in each other's capital. Former U.S. Ambassador David Bruce was named to head the U.S. delegation in Peking.—Ed.

Both sides view bilateral trade as another area from which mutual benefit can be derived, and agreed that economic relations based on equality and mutual benefit are in the interest of the peoples of the two countries. They agree to facilitate the progressive development of trade between their two countries.

Note especially the repeated appearance of the phrase "mutual benefit" and its description of trade between our two countries as developing "progressively." In other contexts the Chinese have talked about our relations, including trade, developing step by step. Implicit in this document is the thought that trade between our two countries has more than just economic significance. Or even if the volume of trade remained statistically microscopic—which is not likely—there are advantages to be derived from focusing attention on it.

If the public eye is drawn to a succession of businessmen, trade groups, and technicians going back and forth between the United States and the People's Republic, this very motion will testify to the existence of an improved relationship and will help create a climate in which cooperation in other areas may become possible.

There are other political advantages accruing to both sides that should not be lightly dismissed. Trade negotiations by private American firms may prove to be an especially significant area for building mutual trust and confidence. Since major political issues are not likely to enter into these discussions, it should be possible to set a positive tone for future discussion of more troublesome matters. By the same token, the acquisition of negotiating skills and techniques can add to one nation's store of information about the other, and thereby ease the way for later negotiations on improvement of political relations.

Moving from these relatively abstract goals to more tangible ones, Peking has undoubtedly calculated the effect of improved trade relations with the United States on its chances for achieving its major policy goals. By trading with the People's Republic, the United States overtly demonstrates its acceptance of the Peking government, even if it does not give it formal recognition. In the speech of a top Chinese leader (Marshal Yeh Chien-ying), delivered on the October 1 National Day celebrations, this theme comes across loud and clear. Even granting some of Peking's outdated perceptions of the nature of the present-day capitalist mind, it is not unreasonable for Chinese leaders to believe that U.S. businessmen who benefit from U.S.-China trade might influence American political opinion in ways that may be mutually beneficial.

By facilitating trade with the United States, Peking also moves toward its goal of diversifying its markets and sources of supply.

Peking undoubtedly calculated that if it can develop new sources of supply for its import requirements, it will never again be so dependent on any single trading partner as to become vulnerable to efforts to exert political pressure through trade. Those who have read Chinese history, as well as the newspaper accounts of China's more recent national experience, will appreciate that the need to be economically independent holds a high priority in China.

To say that political considerations are important is not to suggest, however, that expanding China's trade relations with the United States will not be of mutual economic benefit as well. While the U.S. economy as a whole may not be affected significantly by any foreseeable U.S.-China trade that may develop, specific U.S. industries will benefit. We have already seen this in the recent deals for Boeing aircraft, RCA communications equipment, and wheat; and we may see it again in other industries that can derive important benefits—machine tools, for example, or other sales of aircraft and parts.

Having mentioned these advantages related to expansion of Sino-U.S. trade, I want to inject a note of caution. There are definite constraints placed on rapid expansion of U.S.-China trade by both political and economic considerations. China's reputation as the most revolutionary of the revolutionaries is somewhat offset by its equal renown as one of the most conservative states in international financial dealings. Unlike many of the developing countries that have consciously borrowed heavily in order to finance economic development, the People's Republic has financed its imports either by immediate payment or on ordinary 18-month commercial terms. Even during the most revolutionary phases of its recent history, it preserved its reputation for scrupulous financial dealings. Credits were and are paid off on schedule or even in advance. What this means, of course, is not that the People's Republic has unlimited cash reserves but that it has preferred to limit its imports to the extent of its ability to generate funds through export earnings.

This does not mean that Peking insists on balanced trade with each and every partner; because of its large net export earnings from Hong Kong, it has a certain leeway to accept an unfavorable balance of trade on a bilateral basis with such nations as Japan. Moreover, there have recently been some indications that in special cases the People's Republic may be willing to incur a short-term debt in order to acquire a high-priority item. In general, though, China maintains the principle that it will stand on its own feet. We do not anticipate, therefore, that the People's Republic will choose to incur long-term debt* or allow a significant or prolonged deficit in its balance of trade with another nation.

---

*The February 13, 1973, issue of Japan Economic Journal reported that a group of four Japanese companies, led by Mitsubishi

As long as Peking remains wedded to its policy of self-sufficiency, it is difficult to envision a dramatic increase in the level of foreign trade. The self-sufficiency doctrine has a number of implications for the growth of foreign trade, none of them positive. This philosophy by definition places foreign trade almost in the category of a necessary evil; it can only be an adjunct of domestic economic development whereby China acquires abroad whatever technology and essential goods it cannot produce at home. Because Peking perceives trade in this light, there has been a disinclination to foster the development of export-oriented industries, even if these would afford the People's Republic competitive advantages in the world market. In fact, China has at times in the past turned aside requests to modify its products to make them more marketable in the West. Finally, because the People's Republic remains basically a subsistence agricultural economy, and because all imports are handled through state trading corporations, it is highly unlikely that consumer goods will appear among the priority items in the annual state plan for some time to come.

American businessmen must also consider that the People's Republic has developed well-established trading relationships with low-cost suppliers of its major import needs. Most of its grain comes from Canada or Australia, while capital goods, metals, and fertilizers have been imported from Japanese and Western European suppliers. While it will not be impossible for American firms to break into this market—in fact, given China's desire to diversify its sources of supply, it is likely that some penetration will be accomplished—it would be unrealistic to anticipate major sales at the expense of the Japanese and Western Europeans except in certain high-technology areas.

As long as I am smashing misconceptions about the China market, I might as well destroy another popular myth. I want to emphasize that the People's Republic has established quite a record for pragmatism and flexibility in its business dealings, legends about the strong ideological orientation of the Chinese notwithstanding. Many have probably read reports of Chinese favoritism toward "ideologically correct" firms and refusal to deal with those firms considered to be "reactionary." This has occurred in isolated instances; the Chinese, as they themselves point out, do not separate politics and economics. But within that principle there is room for a considerable degree of

------

Petrochemical Co., will provide China with a five-year deferred payment credit at 6 percent interest for the purchase of an ethylene plant; part of the financing will be extended by the Japanese Export-Import Bank if Japanese commercial banks provide 20 percent of the total price of the plant.—Ed.

flexibility and pragmatism. In most cases, then, I think you will find that Chinese negotiators are more interested in the quality of your product and the size of your market than in your political opinions. What I am suggesting is that there is no advantage for an American businessman to suggest that he supports policies popular in Peking, or that he has been a consistent opponent of some of his own government's policies. Indeed, such an attitude may only serve to place him at a negotiating disadvantage with the Chinese, who do not respect cheap devices for currying favor.

Little research is necessary to unearth confirmation that the Chinese are indeed pragmatic when it comes to business. Up to 1970, only three of the nation's ten largest trading partners had extended diplomatic recognition to Peking. The People's Republic recently concluded a major wheat deal with Australia, even though China's leadership continues to differ with the foreign policy of the Australian government.* When Japanese Premier Kakuei Tanaka arrived in Peking to negotiate the normalization of relations between his country and China, it was evidently made clear to him and other members of his party that continued trade ties with Taiwan would not constitute a barrier in Chinese eyes to a Japan-People's Republic rapprochement. Price and quality, not politics, generally determine the decision for the Chinese negotiators. None of this means, however, that you need not concern yourselves with Chinese sensitivities or that you can engage in political argument without affecting your business prospects. The Chinese are perceptive people who appreciate normal courtesy; they are also quick to detect insincerity.

It seems to me that the great changes that have taken place in our relations with the People's Republic could not have been achieved without certain changes in the attitudes prevailing in both Peking and Washington. For example, it is hardly conceivable that this evolution in our relationship could have occurred at the time of the Great Leap Forward or its aftermath, or during the Cultural Revolution. In other words, it would have been very difficult indeed for these changes to have come about before 1969. Similarly, I am convinced that this breakthrough would not have been possible without the leadership and the commitment that President Nixon has given to the task of ending the period of U.S.-Chinese confrontation.

After 23 years of mutual antagonism and drearily sustained deadlock, the task of persuading the People's Republic to join with us in greatly improving our relations seemed Herculean. Something more than small steps was called for. A dramatic gesture was needed

---

*The reference is to the Liberal Party, which was voted out of office on December 2, 1972.—Ed.

to dispel any suspicions in Peking that our intentions might be directed at short-term domestic political gains or at giving merely the appearance of progress. Despite the risks so often associated with personal diplomacy, the president recognized that the summit approach would best convey to the Chinese his determination to stake the prestige and authority of his presidency on the new policy. Moreover, personal contact at the highest level was necessary to overcome the misunderstandings and myths that had grown up during decades of nondialogue. A new relationship had to be inaugurated on the basis of candor, not evasiveness; on friendly discussion, not glacial silence or steaming rhetoric; and, above all, on growing mutual perceptions that perhaps there was more common ground in our national interests than was apparent from our wide ideological differences. To seize the moment, which could be a fleeting moment, required personal rapport between leaders. The result was the Peking summit meeting.

Developing relations between the United States and the People's Republic during the past few years attest to the success of the Peking summit. Most significantly, the leaders of China seem to have a clearer understanding of U.S. policy and objectives in East Asia. Implementation of the Nixon Doctrine, for example, supplied persuasive evidence that the United States did not, in fact, have designs on China and that it was not seeking to isolate or contain China. On the contrary, it was manifestly our view that the People's Republic should be involved in the international mainstream and that the great problems of our planet could not be resolved without the participation of China in finding solutions and implementing them.

It is not only in terms of U.S.-Chinese relations that the summit was a success, however. As I suggested earlier, the approach to Peking was only a part of a coherent new world view. Perhaps even more significant than the opening of a Chinese-U.S. dialogue was the impression made on other nations. The precedent seemed to make all things possible. Long-time antagonists could approach each other on the basis of shared interests rather than abiding differences. We have seen a series of summit-type meetings between nations, some of which had just barely been on speaking terms, if indeed they had communicated at all. On July 4, 1972, South and North Korea jointly announced that they would need to discuss ways and means of attaining the mutually desired objective of national reunification. As a direct consequence of the Peking summit, there thus seems to have emerged a new pattern of international relations, a new mode of international behavior.

Encouraging as it may be that nations are now competing in image-building and that countries that used to appear intransigent now worry less about appearing tough and more about appearing at least as flexible and conciliatory as their rivals, the millennium is not yet upon us. Serious problems and dangers remain. Yet for the first time in this generation, there is at least the hope that there can develop a pattern of international relationships that can serve the legitimate interests of all nations and a climate in which each nation will see that it is in its interest to pursue its goals by means that do not undermine this new trend.

We proceed on the assumption that no nation is abandoning its goals or what it perceives as its major interests. But there now seems to be a trend among at least the greater powers to pursue their goals through means less likely to involve them in war. In other words, sharp competition will continue to mark relations between nations, and ideologies may not change; but it is to be hoped that in a world of expanded dialogue, trade, and exchanges between nations—even between nations of opposing ideologies—there can be the real beginnings of a lasting peace. President Nixon's trip to Peking made a major contribution to that goal.

CHAPTER

3

THE OVERALL CONTEXT FOR
U.S.-CHINA TRADE RELATIONS
by A. Doak Barnett

The past several years have been a period of historic change
in U.S.-China relations. President Nixon's trip to China was a major
turning point in the development of international affairs, not only
climaxing a period of past change but in many respects marking the
start of a new era. The repercussions of the U.S.-China joint communiqué on the basic pattern of relationships in Asia has already been
extensive. I have no doubt that we will continue to see the effects for
a long time to come.

The Nixon-Chou En-lai summit meeting symbolized the emergence
of a new pattern of multipolar relationships in Asia. It is a pattern
in which there already is—and will continue to be—a much more complicated four-power relationship—among the United States, Japan,
China, and the Soviet Union—than in the past. Not only has this new
pattern required major adjustments in the policies of the four large
powers in the region; every small nation is Asia is in the process of
accommodating to the new situation.

In bilateral U.S.-China relations, the Shanghai joint communiqué
symbolized a dramatic breakthrough. In effect, it ended two decades
of openly hostile confrontation. This does not mean that it resolved
all of the basic problems that have afflicted Sino-American relations.
Most important, the Taiwan problem was really not solved; it was
simply set aside. Nevertheless, the agreements made between President Nixon and Premier Chou En-lai did dramatize the fact that both
Peking and Washington have decided that, even without official diplomatic relations, it is possible, and in fact essential, for the United
States and China to avoid conflict, to work to reduce tensions, and to

Senior fellow, Brookings Institution, Washington, D.C.

try, gradually, to lay the basis for mutual accommodation and an eventual normalization of relations. It is in this context that one must view the first steps that are taking place to develop both trade relations and contacts in a variety of cultural, educational, and scientific fields.

I would like to say, at the start, that I believe the new policy that the United States has adopted toward China is very much in our national interest and deserves the enthusiastic support of Americans of all political persuasions. If anything, it has been long overdue. For many years the majority of China specialists in this country—including myself—have advocated steps of the sort that we have taken during the past several years.

It is important to recognize, however, that despite the dramatic changes that have occurred, there are still many uncertainties about what lies ahead. There are two points that I would like to make right at the start. First of all, the process of "normalizing" relations with China in any full sense is likely to be fairly gradual, and in some respects difficult. There are not likely to be dramatic new breakthroughs in the period immediately ahead. What is realistic to expect is that both sides will take cautious steps in the next few years, within the overall framework established by the Shanghai communiqué, to work toward ultimate "normalization." And in the process of establishing trade and other contacts, each party will try to sound the other out and determine what steps are possible and desirable to increase exchanges of mutual advantage.

It is important that we approach the period ahead with a sense of realism, avoiding the sentimentality and euphoria to which we are prone. For many years the U.S. approach to China has been laden with emotion. Repeatedly the American public has shown a strong propensity to swing from love to hate and back again.

For over two decades after 1949, most Americans tended to view China as public enemy number one—or at least number two—and the general American view of China was obviously distorted. Recently the trend has clearly been in the opposite direction—toward a new love affair. Things Chinese have become a fad, and the tendency of many Americans seems to have been to suspend critical judgment and to view China through a haze of euphoria.

What we currently need is an approach based on neither hate nor sentimentality but, rather, on a dispassionate and objective assessment of China itself and of the opportunities—and problems—of developing a sensible relationship with the Chinese. We are closer, perhaps, to achieving that goal than we were a few years ago; but we certainly have not achieved it yet.

What is the overall context in which we should view China, and the prospects for U.S.-China relations, in the period ahead? First, it is important to recognize that China is experiencing an important transitional period. It is still recovering in many respects from the tremendous upheavals that shook the country during the Cultural Revolution; and it is attempting, in the wake of those upheavals, to build a new leadership and repair its political institutions. In addition, it is poised on the verge of another period of great change and uncertainty that will arrive when Mao dies and the regime has to cope with the difficult problems of succession.

In some respects the situation within China today is confusing. At the grass-roots level, the society and economy are again operating with a fairly high degree of "normalcy" and efficiency, after the shocks of the late 1960s. Yet it is clear that under the surface there are still many serious tensions and unresolved problems that create considerable uncertainty about the future. And in many respects, despite the unprecedented recent flow of American visitors to China, we know relatively little about the real situation in the country—about the way the political system operates, who the leaders are, and how decisions are made.

It is not possible here to go into any great detail about the situation, so the following comments will focus on four major problem areas and trends affecting them. How the Chinese leadership copes with these problems will determine in many respects the main course of events in China in the next few years, and the results will shape the basic context for the developing U.S.-China relationship.

One of the fundamental problems that China now faces is in leadership. In some respects the present leadership in Peking is now showing remarkable skill and effectiveness. A great deal of the credit must go to one man, Chou En-lai. But there is considerable evidence to suggest that in a basic sense the top leadership in China is still relatively fragile and in some respects narrowly based. It is probably still inherently unstable to some degree. This fact alone, obviously, creates very considerable uncertainty about the future.

During the first decade and a half of the Communist rule in China, the top leadership that ran the regime constituted one of the most stable groups in the world. United by a strong consensus, the tightly knit leaders who led the Communists to victory in the Revolution held together to a remarkable degree in the years that followed. Only a handful were purged during the first decade and a half.

During the Cultural Revolution, however, the unity of the leadership was shattered. Over half of the men at the top were purged by Mao, and leaders at regional and local levels were affected almost as greatly. In 1969, when the Cultural Revolution drew to a close, a new leadership group was put together; but it has proved to be both fragile and unstable. Roughly half of its members—in the Politburo and Central Committee—have subsequently disappeared from view.

To date the regime has had great difficulty in trying to put together a new, broadly based, stable leadership. A handful of men in
Peking appears to be running the show. Mao remains in possession
of ultimate power—a brooding presence in the background whose
endorsement is necessary if any policy is to be successful—but his
role has seemed to become less and less active over time. Chou
En-lai is clearly the man in actual charge of day-to-day affairs and
is shaping the country's policies both at home and abroad, with the
help of a coterie of close associates: Li Hsien-nien in economics and
domestic affairs generally, Yeh Chien-ying in military affairs, and
some able second-ranking proteges of Chou's in foreign affairs.

There is still a group in the top leadership representing the
"radicals" who were in the ascendancy during the Cultural Revolution;
they include Mao's wife, Chiang Ching, Yao Wen-yuan, and the top
political leader in Shanghai, Chang Ch'un-ch'ao. Also in the top leadership group are some extremely influential regional military leaders
who survived the sweeping purge of the central military hierarchy
in 1971: they include Ch'en Hsi-lien in Manchuria and Hsu Shih-yu
in Central China. It is difficult to know the extent to which any real
consensus unites these groups. Until recently the top leadership has
been notably lacking in the kind of Communist Party organization men,
economic planners and administrators, and specialists of all sorts
who were so prominent before the Cultural Revolution. The problem
that the regime still faces, therefore, is how to broaden and strengthen
the leadership, build a genuine consensus once again, and then, at
some time in the not-too-distant future, try to manage the succession
process at the time of Mao's death without damaging conflict.

When Mao dies, no single individual is likely to be able to succeed
him in any real sense. The regime will doubtless try to build a new
kind of collective leadership; but if it is to be effective, it will certainly have to be more broadly based than the group now at the top in
Peking.

If Chou En-lai continues to play a central role in the leadership
after Mao's death, there is a reasonably good chance that he will be
able to build a viable collective leadership and manage the succession
and post-Mao transition fairly smoothly. There can be no certainty
about this, however. In fact, there is no certainty that he will outlive
Mao—and this fact poses a large question mark for the future.

A second major problem facing the regime in China today centers
on the need to reestablish a workable, viable relationship between the
military and civilian leaderships. In the early years of the Communist
regime, China's leaders were remarkably successful in this regard.
Although the Party's revolutionary armies spearheaded the Communist take-over in 1949, the transition to civilian rule thereafter
was made both rapidly and smoothly; and in the 1950s the Chinese

Communist military establishment withdrew to a large extent from civilian administration and political affairs and concentrated on modernization and national defense. This trend began to be reversed, however, when Mao insisted on repoliticizing the army and then turned to it for support against his political enemies in the Communist Party bureaucracy.

Finally, during the Cultural Revolution a radical change in military-civil relations occurred. During 1967-68, when the Communist Party and civilian bureaucracies were paralyzed, there was a gaping vacuum that the army filled. Starting in 1967, military men moved into dominant political positions throughout much of China. In Peking, Lin Piao was designated Mao's successor; and at regional and local levels, political commanders and commissars took charge almost everywhere.

This was obviously an extremely abnormal situation, and an eventual swing of the pendulum back toward greater civilian control was inevitable. It came, however, sooner than most observers expected. In 1971 there was a major crisis in civil-military relations in China. Lin Piao and the entire top military hierarchy were purged, and China's civilian leaders took various steps to try to cut back the political influence and roles of the army. Despite this purge—or perhaps in part because of it—the present state of relationships between China's civilian and military leaders is still uncertain. Military men are more in the background than they were a few years ago; but it is obvious that they still hold great power, especially at the local level. At the center the key positions in the national military establishment remain unfilled, and it is impossible to say who is really running the military establishment or the degree to which a stable situation has emerged.

Looking to the future, if China is to manage the succession process without excessively disruptive conflict, its top civilian and military leaders will have to work out a new pattern of relationships; and this will require compromises on both sides. The military establishment will be under pressure to accept civilian primacy, but China's civilian leaders cannot avoid accommodating to the fact that the army still exercises great power in many parts of the country. But no one can say for certain whether such compromises will prevent disruptive conflict. If they do, the post-Mao transition in China may be fairly smooth. If not, China could—at worst—experience another period of great internal strife and turmoil, as a result of which military men might well emerge in dominant political positions once again.

A third major problem that the Chinese Communists now face is the kind of economic development strategy they should pursue in the years immediately ahead. Ever since the 1950s, there have been significant divisions within Chinese leadership between those who have favored a "Maoist" strategy—stressing mass mobilization, rapid "leaps," and priority for egalitarian values—and those who have favored a more orderly and gradual development, centralized bureaucratic management, and stress on economic growth per se rather than on ideological goals and other social values. The Maoist vision, in its most extreme form, underlay the Great Leap Forward. Instead of getting China "over the hump" in its economic development, however, as Mao obviously hoped, it resulted in an extremely serious economic depression in the early 1960s. Thereafter, the pendulum swung quite far toward relatively pragmatic, nonideological, and non-Maoist policies.

In the last few years the general economic development strategy that appears to have been emerging in China obviously represents a complex mixture of Maoist and non-Maoist features. It is a strategy that has much to be said for it. It emphasizes national self-reliance, substantial decentralization of decision-making, special attention to agriculture, small-scale local industries, improvement of education and health in the countryside, and sizable transfers of both people and resources from urban to rural areas. The regime has in some respects approached many of its economic problems in a fairly realistic and pragmatic fashion. Instead of attempting any new "great leap," it has worked for steady, incremental change. Instead of mobilizing the population as it did in the late 1950s, it has again put primary stress on the need to restore rational planning and management. And although it continues to focus its propaganda on the need to realize Mao's egalitarian values, it has in practice maintained—and even increased—concrete material incentives in order to spur hard work and greater efficiency.

During the height of the Cultural Revolution, the Chinese economy, and in particular its industrial sector, suffered a new setback that, while nothing like the one following the Great Leap Forward, was nevertheless significant. Since 1969, however, recovery has been rapid; and it is clear that China today is again enjoying a period of growth—perhaps the most significant growth since the 1950s. But it remains to be seen whether the present policies that the regime is pursuing will result in a sustained process of development at a rate sufficient to satisfy China's leaders, and whether the conflicts over economic strategy that divided the leadership in the pre-Cultural Revolution period have really been resolved.

The extent to which China in the next few years increases its involvement in the world economy—and tries to expand its foreign trade-will depend very much on what its broad economic development strategy is at home. As long as it continues to place primary stress on self-reliance, the overall level of China's foreign trade is likely to remain relatively small, no matter how skillful or flexible Chinese leaders are in managing foreign trade. As of 1971, China's foreign trade—at a level of about $4.5 billion a year—was one of the lowest in per capita terms for any major nation; in 1972 it had risen to over $5 billion, only slightly greater than it was in the late 1950s. In the period ahead trade will certainly grow, but it would be unrealistic to expect any very rapid expansion unless and until there is a major change in Chinese attitudes and policies and overall domestic development strategy.

Finally, a fourth very broad area in which one can raise many questions about future Chinese problems and policies is foreign policy. It is in this area that some of the most dramatic changes in China have occurred in recent years. It is easy to forget that it was not very long ago that China, during the Cultural Revolution, appeared to be opting out of world affairs. Verbally, its policies at that time were extremely militant, although in reality China drew into a shell and was extraordinarily isolationist.

Today the picture is very different. Under Chou En-lai's skillful direction, China has been developing notably flexible, pragmatic— and one could also say moderate—policies abroad, designed to expand China's diplomatic and political roles in the international community in almost every possible way.

There are probably many factors that help to explain this new approach. Broad security considerations, however, are doubtless the crucial ones. For several years one of the greatest preoccupations of leaders in Peking has been a genuine fear that they might be confronted by a serious threat from the Soviet Union.

In addition, the Chinese leaders, like those in most other major capitals, have finally recognized that bipolarity is a thing of the past and that we live in a very multipolar world. Basic considerations of this sort have led the Chinese to conclude that greater flexibility on their part is now essential. It is in this context that the breakthrough in U.S.-China relations must be viewed. It is a result, in part, of a much broader change in China's foreign policy growing out of international trends toward a multipolar world.

One of the crucial questions that must be asked in looking ahead is whether one should assume that China's present general approach to the outside world is likely to continue for a considerable period of time. It must immediately be said that one cannot be certain that it will. China has shifted its overall strategy in foreign relations several times since 1949, and it could certainly do so again. Moreover, there is evidence that Chou En-lai has had to overcome some internal opposition in China to the new policies that he has pursued—and in particular his new policy toward the United States. No one can be absolutely sure, therefore, what will happen when Mao and Chou pass from the scene.

Nevertheless, there is reason to believe that China's current broad strategy in foreign affairs is likely to continue without basic change for a considerable period, even if there are important leadership changes in China. The most important reason this is likely is that the foreign policy China is now pursuing is a realistic response to fundamental changes in the broad pattern of international relations in Asia, and reflects important security, economic, and other interests in ways that are not likely to change soon.

If this is, in fact, the case, what does it mean for U.S.-China relations in the period ahead? I believe it means that we can expect the Chinese to continue to work toward a gradual accommodation and normalization of relations with the United States, even though—to repeat what I said at the start—the process is likely to be gradual rather than rapid and progress is likely to come in relatively small steps taken by both sides rather than as a result of dramatic new breakthroughs.

To return to the question of trade, how are these external and internal political developments likely to affect the prospects for U.S.-China economic exchange in the period immediately ahead? First of all, how well China is able to cope with the problems discussed above—the problems of leadership and succession, military-civil relations, and economic development—will go far toward shaping the kind of regime China has and the foreign policies it pursues in the next few years, particularly in the post-Mao era. I am inclined to believe that China's post-Mao leaders will probably continue to look outward and to try, to the best of their ability, to expand their world role diplomatically and politically. It is more doubtful, however, that they will decide completely to abandon self-reliance in order to involve China much more in the world economy.

If this is true, it means that China trade will continue to be relatively small, at least in comparison with that of the major trading nations, and that U.S. businessmen interested in China trade will be competing for a slice of what will probably continue to be a relatively small pie. How large a slice Americans may be able to obtain will depend on various factors, both economic and political. There is little doubt that China will want to buy, in the next few years, certain high-technology goods from the United States. Airplanes are obviously a notable example. But for there to be any rapid increase in U.S.-China trade, the Chinese would either have to expand their overall foreign trade substantially or to shift some of their present trade from other countries, such as Japan and Germany, to the United States.

In sum, it is realistic to expect that U.S.-China trade will grow, but at a relatively modest rate. I believe that any U.S.-China trade is important—not simply to the American business interests involved but in terms of the broad goal of developing contacts with the Chinese and working toward an improved overall relationship. We should do everything we can, therefore, to put this trade on a solid basis and to expand it as much as possible. But it is important to view the prospects realistically; and if one assesses the possibilities in the context of the broad political as well as economic factors that will affect future trends, one should expect a significant growth of trade but recognize that many factors will continue to limit its size.*

---

*Since the above was written, U.S.-China trade has developed faster than most observers anticipated—from a starting point that was near zero. Two-way trade in 1972 exceeded $90 million. By the end of 1973, it appeared likely to be more than $1 billion for the year. This increase was due in large part to China's purchase from the United States of airplanes, grain, and cotton, however; and the development of diversified, broadly based, two-way exchanges is still in an early stage. The factors and problems discussed above will almost certainly continue to impose several limits on the overall level of U.S.-China trade. However, the general trends—and such steps as the establishment of liaison offices in Peking and Washington and of the National Council on U.S.-China Trade in the United States—indicate that significant progress is being made in consolidating the overall U.S.-China relationship and in establishing a basis for mutually beneficial, if limited, trade.

4

A HISTORICAL OVERVIEW OF U.S.-CHINA ECONOMIC RELATIONS
by Harned P. Hoose

The 30 men and 4 women who went from the United States to Canton seeking trade in April and May of 1972 were the first American business people to enter China's mainland since 1949. While the Americans' trip to the Canton Fair was a pioneering undertaking in one sense, in another sense it marked the reopening of long-established Sino-American business contacts, the origins of which date back almost 200 years.

It was in 1784, only a few months after the conclusion of the American Revolution, that a Yankee sailing clipper, the Emperor of China, loaded with a cargo of furs and hides, worked its way past what is now Hong Kong, up the Pearl River, to the Chinese trading port of Canton.

The log of this journey contains the following:

> . . . they are a set of as respectable men as are com-
> monly found in other ports of the world. They are
> intelligent, exact accountants, punctual in their engage-
> ments, and . . . value themselves much upon maintaining
> a fair character.

The Chinese reports of the visit were equally friendly. They noted that the Americans were honest, hard-working, and fair in their dealings.

That first business contact in 1784 was followed by 165 years of trade and commerce between the two peoples. There were some

---

Attorney-at-law, Los Angeles; consulting professor, international business, Graduate School of Business Administration, University of Southern California.

unpleasant episodes, of course; but on the whole, American-Chinese relations over this long period, which ended in 1949, were characterized by friendship and by respect. The goodwill of each nation for the other found expression in the joint establishment of educational institutions and hospitals, and in the launching of various programs of mutual benefit, including exchanges of students, famine relief, and cultural missions.

The end of all this in 1949 evoked a hostile comment by Chairman Mao Tse-tung, entitled "Farewell, J. Leighton Stewart." Stewart, the last U.S. ambassador to China prior to the rupture of relations in 1949, had been born and raised in China. He had devoted his entire life to China, had been a noted educator before assuming the ambassadorship, and deeply loved the Chinese people. Chairman Mao acknowledged that in his essay but bitterly charged that Stewart and other Americans in China had been guilty of "spiritual and educational aggression." Twenty-three years of mutual exclusion and bitterness followed.

Then, in a series of brilliant and carefully executed moves between July 1969 and February 1972, President Nixon lifted the American embargo on things Chinese, and China reciprocated by significantly widening the crack in its bamboo curtain.

When President Nixon and his party touched down at Peking's airport in February 1972, the old and historic road to China was reopened. A few hours later, "Farewell, J. Leighton Stewart" was replaced by Chairman Mao's welcome to the American president. And with the Shanghai joint communiqué ensued the resumption, at least in some degree, of the historic commercial and cultural links between the Americans and the Chinese.

The relevant part of the communiqué provided:

> Both sides view bilateral trade as another area from
> which mutual benefit can be derived, and agreed that
> economic relations based on equality and mutual bene-
> fit are in the interest of the peoples of the two countries.
> They agree to facilitate the progressive development of
> trade between their two countries.

Because the Chinese have stressed during their trade negotiations with the Americans that any trade will be conducted pursuant to the Shanghai joint communiqué, and since the document's terms are used by Chinese negotiators both as a sword and as a shield during negotiations, it is important to pay close heed to the text agreed upon by President Nixon and Premier Chou En-lai. The first sentence dealing with trade provides: "Both sides view bilateral trade as another area from which mutual benefit can be derived. . . ." Notice that the two governments exchanged a view—not an agreement. Views are easily changed or withdrawn. Further, observe the word "bilateral." There is to be no one-sided profiting from trade, the Chinese insist. There must be reciprocity. Next, the stress on mutual benefit is to be studied. The Chinese were asserting their concern here that the United States might seek what the Chinese regard as neocolonial plundering, or transactions of benefit only to America.

Another significant phrase in the communiqué is ". . . and agreed that economic relations based on equality and mutual benefit are in the interest of the peoples of the two countries." This concern for equal treatment is no doubt grounded partly on fear of American economic and military strength and partly on a reading of the history of Western dealings with China under what the Chinese regard as the "unequal treaties."

It is now appropriate to examine the rules under which the serious business of Sino-American trade is to be played: the procedures, the strategies, the tactics and techniques that may be appropriately used by American traders in the China trade, and the nature and extent of the financial stakes of such trade. It is necessary also to consider the competitors in this trade and how others—the Europeans and the non-Chinese Asians—stand in the financial pennant race for China's trade dollars.

The very first question must be whether there is a market for U.S. products and, if so, whether it is sufficiently large to warrant our efforts. On this point we must distinguish between what China has been economically and financially, what it is now, and what it has the capacity and determination to become.

Historically, China has not been a substantial trader. Statistics for the six years predating President Nixon's visit published by the Department of State and the Department of Commerce make this very evident.

Foreign Trade of the People's Republic of China

	Exports	Imports
1966	$2.2 billion	$2.0 billion
1967	1.9	1.9
1968	1.9	1.8
1969	2.0	1.8
1970	2.0	2.2
1971	2.3	2.2

Such statistics do not indicate a very large market for U.S. products, even assuming (which is unrealistic) that we can immediately or entirely replace China's long-established trading partners, such as

Japan, Hong Kong, Singapore, West Germany, and the United Kingdom. Furthermore, China at present is an agricultural economy, with an annual per capita income of approximately $145. Finally, China has made it clear that it will not use credit devices in its international trade. This limits its purchases to available funds generated by its exports.

Even under the assumptions (a) that our relationships with China continue to improve and expand, and (b) that we can succeed in competition with China's European and non-Chinese Asiatic trading partners, the figures suggest that China is not a market worthy of the effort, the expenses, and the hazards of seeking trade with it.

But if these conclusions are warranted, why did Canada spend about $1 million in underwriting the Canadian Exhibit in Peking? Why, if China is not a good market, did Japan rush to open diplomatic relations with China, at some risk to its trade and investments with Taiwan? And why are the Italians, the French, the English, the Scandinavians, the East European nations, and practically the entire world of traders sending trade missions to Peking, holding trade exhibitions there, entering into trade agreements with Peking, and otherwise struggling for a place in line or, if possible, at the head of the line, to sell to the People's Republic of China?

Finally, we may ask why so many U.S. companies are clamoring at China's gates for admission. Has everyone become so romantic about a newly opening market, so excited at the new dialogue with the Chinese, that pragmatic business judgment has given way to a passion for Chinese food, or acupuncture, or sight-seeing at the Great Wall?

The answer is that China's statistics relate to the past, not to the future. And the future, based on present trends, is likely to differ radically from the past. Specifically, the Chinese are determined to procure increasing amounts of modern technology and to combine this technology with the characteristic Chinese determination and team spirit in a kind of new industrial revolution.

The most recent figures for U.S.-China trade are beginning to reflect this profoundly changed attitude. Thus, in April 1972 about 34 Americans attended the Canton Trade Fair; in October 1972 approximately 75 Americans attended; and in April-May 1973, there were about 150 of us at the fair. This increase in business contacts was accompanied by a marked increase in the value of deals consummated. In 1971 recorded trade between the United States and the People's Republic amounted to only $5 million, a tiny fraction of China's total trade. In 1972 trade both ways increased to $90 million ($60 million in U.S. exports to China, $30 million in U.S. purchases from China).

The U.S. government's original estimate of trade (both ways) between China and the United States in 1973 was $300 million. That estimate, however, was exceeded in the first six months of the year. Some revised U.S. estimates of the volume of trade for all of 1973 go as high as $850 million for the total of exports and imports. The Chinese themselves have estimated that the 1973 figure will reach $1 billion. It is worth noting also that since the resumption of trade between the two countries, the United States has vaulted from last on the list of China's trading partners to a tie for third place (after Japan and Hong Kong and equal to West Germany). Even more startling, I was told by responsible officials in the People's Republic in 1972 that they fully expected their trade with the United States to approach $5 billion annually (exports and imports combined) within five to eight years. Similar estimates were given to me in the spring of 1973 when I was in China.

There are three reasons for being optimistic about China's economic future; and hence about prospects for increased trade:

1. China has succeeded to a remarkable degree in feeding, clothing, housing, healing, and otherwise caring for its vast population; and for the most part the people are willing and eager to march to China's current drums.

2. Having essentially solved its physical problems relating to human survival and basic needs, China is now ready, psychologically and economically, to concentrate upon technological development, including the establishment and maintenance of heavy industry and the manufacture of sophisticated equipment for essentially nonconsumer-oriented production (including further development of iron and steel production, machine tools, automated lathes, computers, transport, mining, and petroleum).

3. China is determined to accelerate its program by buying heavily from the West, from Japan, and from any nation with sophisticated machinery and know-how, except the Soviet Union. China's determination stems from two central stimuli:

a. Grave concern with the threat posed by the Soviet Union, its relatively advanced technology, and the 1 million men, the armor, the rockets, and other military installations on its border with China. The Soviet-Chinese relationship has seriously deteriorated; China has suffered a number of Soviet shocks in recent years that make Japan's so-called "Nixon shocks" mild by comparison. These include the border clashes and the enormous troop movements on China's northern and western borders. The Chinese leaders have decided that there is no time for the gradual development of China's defenses; China's industrial revolution must be accelerated immediately. That is one of the major reasons why China has contracted for several Concordes, is buying $125 million worth of Boeing planes, has acquired two RCA satellite ground stations, and is shopping widely for similarly sophisticated items.

b. Japan's phenomenal economic growth is viewed with alarm by China. It has watched Japan become an economic giant on China's doorstep, it has seen Japan expand financially throughout Asia, and it feels that it cannot permit the Japanese expansion to proceed unchallenged. China feels that Japan might revert to militarism at any time, and that this poses a serious threat to China's security.

Do these judgments imply another disastrous Great Leap Forward? They do not. There is a new element of economic and political realism in the grand strategy the Chinese are now designing. And a very large place is reserved for foreign trade in the new strategy. If China is afraid of the Soviet Union, and if it does not wish to become overly reliant upon Japan, who is available for the trade China wants? The answer is Western Europe; Eastern Europe; the United Kingdom and related nations, such as Australia, New Zealand, and Canada; other Asian nations; and the United States. Considering what China wants to buy, we have an exceptionally good shot at the market because of our special abilities and capacities to design and produce technically sophisticated products.

So there are the need and the desire. What of China's capacity to pay for what she wants?

1. The Oil and Gas Journal of December 13, 1971, states that China had crude oil reserves of 2.729 billion tons at the end of 1971, which is equal to 3.27 percent of the world's oil reserves.* China holds 12th place in the world as far as proven oil reserves are concerned. American and European sources admit that the above data omit any possible offshore oil reserves and that the data are based on fragmentary information. Chinese sources have informed me that they believe that China is oil-rich, with enormous reserves in the Gobi Desert areas, in the Northeast, and under the sea along the northeast coast.

True or not, the Chinese are convinced that they have vast oil and gas reserves. They are buying very sophisticated equipment and machinery for oil and gas exploration, extraction, and refining. And they are not inept in this field. Since 1966, China has been wholly self-sufficient in petroleum and produces its own aviation fuel in quantities large enough to supply their small but growing air fleet.

If China is already self-sufficient in oil, why is it interested in oil and gas exploration? It is important to note that China can become an oil-exporting nation. If the reserves are even a fraction of what is claimed, it is clear that in a matter of a few years China may be in a position to use its earnings from oil and gas exports to import foreign goods in significantly larger quantities than at present.

---

*The April 1973 issue of World Oil (Gulf Publishing Co.), p. 94, estimates that China has 19.6 billion barrels of oil reserves.—Ed.

I wish also to report (and the facts have been confirmed informally by the U.S. State and Commerce Departments) that massive petroleum-related negotiations are quite advanced between China and some U.S. corporations. It is further worthy of note that the recent Japanese mission to China (under the leadership of Prime Minister Kakuei Tanaka) included petroleum and mineral specialists. Japanese industrial groups involved in economic studies of the People's Republic have estimated that Japan's potential for trade with China, including trade in petroleum products, is on the order of $5 billion per annum over the next decade.

2. China is rich in a number of minerals. For example, it is widely known that China's deposits of antimony and tungsten are the largest in the world. It is also well-endowed with ferrous metals and coal. These too can become a primary source of funding of China's foreign trade.

3. China's exports are even now not inconsiderable, and are obviously large enough to generate the several hundred million dollars needed to conclude the purchase deals with Boeing, RCA, and others whose transactions are now in the negotiations process. Recent large grain and related purchases by China have involved large sums of cash and relatively short-term payouts. China's United Nations headquarters in New York was bought for about $4 million in cash, for instance. In sum, the Chinese have shown a remarkable capacity to generate hard dollars in international trade. At the same time, it is clear that, in the short term anyway, China's cash resources will not be sufficient to pay for the massive purchases of sophisticated machinery and equipment needed to make the new industrial revolution in that country a reality. This leads naturally to a consideration of the possibility that China's hitherto negative attitude toward acceptance of international credit may change.

4. China is actively studying various international credit and financing devices, even while it insists that any such transactions would not be acceptable. That may be the present policy, but this does not preclude the possibility of its resorting to foreign credit in the future.

5. Again, while it is unlikely at present that China will embark upon some form of joint venture with European, Japanese, or U.S. entities, it is always possible that China will entertain such ideas provided the international situation warrants it and provided that China can retain full title to the facilities and the products, with some arrangement for compensation to the other joint venturer (say an arrangement to recoup expenditures, followed by a sharing of the proceeds for a few years).

6. Finally, three- or four-party or even multiparty barter is a growing possibility. Such techniques have been employed

successfully in recent years in trade between Western and East European countries.

The Chinese are convinced, the Japanese are convinced, and many of our European competitors are convinced that China is likely to purchase substantial quantities of imports in the future. It is my view that our competitors' evaluations are accurate, and that China is a great new market. But China is in the process of choosing its trading partners today, and these decisions will yield their fruits within the next few years.

How should an American corporation proceed to penetrate the China market? The following steps are suggested:

1. Examine your products in relation to China's needs. On the latter point the U.S. Department of Commerce has some good data. Additional materials are available through a number of other governmental and educational sources. Consumer goods are not currently needed by China, but advanced and sophisticated capital equipment and technology are urgently needed and are high on China's shopping list.

2. Undertake a mail campaign, directed to the applicable China state trading company. Send cover letters in English, together with catalogs, pictures, corporate data (including your annual report), and materials generally introducing your company and its products. You can launch this campaign on your own. More than 23,000 American businessmen did so in connection with the spring 1972 Canton Trade Fair. Some 36 of those 23,000 succeeded in attracting China's interest sufficiently to gain entry to the fair and to China. Additionally, of course, you can obtain specialized assistance for your campaign from various sources, including American and non-American consultants who have succeeded in helping corporations gain access to Chinese officials.

3. Presentations of your products in Hong Kong may help. Some U.S. companies have found it useful to call on the China representatives in their Hong Kong offices, located in the China Resources Company in the Bank of China building in Hong Kong. While many Western buyers have successfully used this route, on the whole it has not been very successful for Western sellers.

4. In your mail campaign, be courteous but do not chafe or remonstrate when you do not receive replies. Keep the campaign going. Be patient. Be persistent. Communicate every few months.

5. Try to obtain an invitation to the Canton Trade Fair. Apply directly to the fair via mail, and also to the Chinese trading company with jurisdiction over your products. If you become one of the fortunate few, of the thousands who apply, to receive an invitation to the Canton Trade Fair, this can launch your business with China. Or you can gain access by proxy, by having one of the European, Asiatic, or

American individuals or firms who have received invitations represent your company in China or at the fair.

6. If and when your invitation from China materializes, prepare for very long negotiations, both in time between sessions and in the length of sessions. The Chinese are courteous, prompt, and keep their word in business dealings. But they negotiate at great length. You must prepare yourself well with respect to your products, your competitors' products, and the world market in your field. The Chinese will require accurate and detailed information. You must also be prepared to show the Chinese how your products will benefit the Chinese people.

7. Both nations have now established liaison offices in each other's capital. The U.S. team in Peking includes two very able economic and trade experts, Herb Horowitz, the senior commercial officer, and Bill Rope, who is associated with Horowitz. They are addressing themselves to, among other things, such important matters as China's desire to have most-favored-nation status extended to it by the United States (for example, Chinese glass, which is produced very efficiently and which is in short supply in the United States, carries a U.S. duty rate about twice as high as glass imports from most other countries). Similarly, the Chinese have sent highly qualified men to their liaison office, which is in the Mayflower Hotel, 1127 Connecticut Ave., N.W., Washington, D.C. They include Huang Chen, who directs the office, and his colleague Chang Chien-hua.

For those who wish direct counseling by American officials on China trade, the following agencies are recommended:

a. The China desk of the East-West Bureau of the U.S. Department of Commerce, which aggressively seeks leads to business potential in China for Americans; interviews all returned traders; surveys the market; and responds promptly to requests for information. Helpful sets of printed materials are available from this source.

b. The China desk at the U.S. State Department provides similar information but with more stress on broader economic aspects and trends, as well as on cultural and political institutions that may affect American businessmen.

c. The newly formed National Council for U.S.-China Trade, Post Office Box 2804, Washington, D.C., 20013.

The path to trade with China is long and difficult, but it is now open. Many in China and in the West feel that soon the path will become a road, and then a great highway of trade between China and the rest of the world. It is a highway not only to trade but also to peaceful relations between China and the United States. And it is well worth the journey.

II

THE CHINESE ECONOMY: RESOURCES, NEEDS, POTENTIAL

MAINLAND CHINA:
THE ECONOMY BEHIND
THE OPENING DOOR
by Robert F. Dernberger

The purpose of this chapter is to provide a summary view of the domestic Chinese economy. Insofar as China's foreign trade is concerned, I make an implicit assumption: Chinese foreign trade is not a separate economic activity but a reflection of domestic economic activity and decisions. Thus, although China's foreign trade is relatively small in absolute terms, compared with domestic economic activity, and is a state-run activity, that trade, like the trade of other countries, reflects developments within the domestic economy.

In reviewing the highlights of the domestic economy, I need to present three caveats. First, most who do research on the economy of China face the dilemma of making guesses and intuitive judgments on the basis of very limited facts. Very few bits and pieces of evidence often have been used to build castles. The factual evidence is relatively limited for building a very strong case for any specific quantitative argument.

A second real problem lies in the attempt to predict future actions on the basis of past actions. This is an especially crucial problem in the case of China. Because we know so little about the past, it is even more difficult to predict the future. Furthermore, it is not easy to identify the political leadership in China and its policies. Thus the problem of determining China's future domestic policy is a very risky venture. I agree with those who believe the Chinese have adopted and are following a rational policy in pursuit of economic development, especially in the area of foreign trade. David Wilson has argued that the Chinese are on a path of stability. In much the same vein, I would

Associate professor of economics and member of Executive Committee, Center for Chinese Studies, University of Michigan, Ann Arbor.

argue that they are on the path of rationality. Because that could be debated, and debated very heatedly, let me present a brief argument in my defense that concerns developments in the recent past.

Although the Cultural Revolution has been cited as evidence of irrational exercise of power by the Chinese, I think they were very successful during the Cultural Revolution in insulating the economy from serious disruption, especially in such crucial areas as the military industries. Furthermore, not only were they successful in protecting the domestic economy, they have recently engaged in the elimination of the ultra-Left. The ultra-Left rose to a position of significant power as an aftermath of the Cultural Revolution, but it is being replaced by the more moderate leaders. In any event, I am a strong believer in their rationality and feel that they will be rational in the foreseeable future.

Another caveat that has to be made explicit is the embarassing need to simplify and generalize about a very complex, highly diverse economy. For example, there are five main agricultural areas in China: the Manchurian plain, the Yellow River (North China) plain, the delta around Shanghai, the Szechuan basin, and the river delta around Canton. The Manchurian plain produces soybeans; the North China plain, wheat; the Shanghai delta, cotton; double-cropping, wet-rice plots and tea cultivation are located near Canton; and the Szechuan basin is China's rice and fruit bowl. These are distinct areas of the China where the bulk of the Chinese people live and engage in agricultural production.

When you turn to industry, there are the old—some would say imperialist—areas of Shanghai and Manchuria and the newer areas, such as Lanchow, Paotao, and Wu Han, which are key centers of modern economic activity. These industrial urban areas are separated by very long distances and transport costs are high. Thus, when we simplify China as a single economy, it often does violence to the facts. In addition, there is a a very serious temporal problem. China has been plagued with what economists call the investment-policy cycle found in most Communist countries.

This cycle stems from the fact that investment decisions in Communist countries are political decisions, and they tend to be bunched according to whether the economic climate is very optimistic or pessimistic. Once investment decisions are bunched, there is a built-in investment-induced cycle. In a Communist country it is not a million firms, but a single government, making investment decisions. This means there is a severe cycle in total investment that results in an even greater cycle in final output. This cycle is made even worse by the fact that a Communist economic system does not have the built-in, self-correcting tendencies that can be found in market economies to smooth out these waves in economic activity.

44

For example, if private businessmen find their inventories changing or their markets softening, they will take action to correct this tendency. In a Communist country, where many of the decisions are political, they can continue in effect beyond the normal state of disequilibrium because political power has intruded into the economy. While China has experienced a very severe case of this cycle, I will discuss the economy as if it were located in one spot, at one point in time, so as to emphasize the fundamental problems involved.

The best way to begin a discussion of China's economy is to argue that China is an exemplary case of an underdeveloped country. China has a very large population with very limited fertile land, and the bulk of the population lives in villages scattered on that land. Productivity per man is low and per capita income is very low. That, I believe, is the definition of underdevelopment.

China's economy also provides an excellent case study of the economic development problem inasmuch as China has a leadership group dedicated to doing something about the problem. Moreover, they have the power and the ability to do something about it. They are not always wise in the policies they adopt, but they do discuss and put into effect a host of economic policies and genuinely seek to make them succeed. This is in direct contrast with several other under-developed countries.

Unfortunately, however, because of limited information and the language barrier, economists tend to ignore China. They study it either because they are Soviet specialists and want to look at China as a special case of the Soviet model, or because they are China specialists and want to look at a very important aspect of China's evolution. Development economists, in general, look at Africa, South America, India, and other areas of the world as case studies of economic development. In any event, China is there to be studied; and I would hope more economists would study it, since it does provide an excellent example of the classical problem of economic development.

What is the key to understanding the underdevelopment problem? I believe it is the ratio of agricultural output to population, and this is the first figure to examine when considering the economic problem in an underdeveloped country. Moreover, it is not just the ratio, but its rate of change that is of interest to economists.

To understand China's problem, therefore, let's look at the numerator first. Agricultural output was the neglected stepchild of the Chinese Communist attempt at economic development in the 1950s, and a relatively small share of investment was devoted to that sector. Rather, the Chinese believed they could rely upon normative campaigns in urging the people to greater productive efforts with a rapid re-organization of the agricultural sector.

45

The first step in the reorganization of agriculture was the mutual aid teams—a traditional Chinese organization in agricultural production. After mutual aid teams had been started, they began to develop elementary producers' cooperatives, in which the peasants pooled their land, labor, and capital and were paid for them. These cooperatives made a good deal of sense in Chinese agriculture, which consisted of very limited holdings and had very limited sources of outside capital. Once the landlord had been eliminated and the state was unwilling to put large sums of money into the agricultural sector, some sort of cooperative organization to bring about agricultural development was required.

No sooner had elementary producers' cooperatives begun to be formed, however, than the impatient Maoists argued for a rapid transition to advanced producers' cooperatives—in which the peasant was paid for his labor but not for his land and his capital. The land and capital became the property of the cooperative. This still made some sense in Chinese agriculture because it was organized around the village structure in the countryside—on land and with people the peasant knew. However, the movement toward the commune, a further step toward true socialism, was toward an organizational form alien to traditional Chinese social and economic organization.

The commune organized the Chinese peasant into a production unit of about 25,000 members, beyond the scope of his normal friendships and terms of reference. In addition, he was organized into work teams that were moved about to perform various jobs, including nonagricultural jobs. Thus the peasant became divorced from his land and from his friends within an excessively large decision-making unit. The commune did not work and ended in failure because it erred in putting decision-making in agriculture beyond the reach of those who were actually engaged in production. It also relied upon payments in kind not related to the work done, and it eliminated the private plots. Thus, the peasant became totally transformed into a wage earner whose wage was not directly relevant to what he did.

Inasmuch as the decision-making and motivational aspects of the commune were not very productive, they led to the downfall of the organization. One must add, of course, that the very bad weather in 1959 was an additional negative factor leading to a severe agricultural crisis in 1959-61. The important thing, however, was that once the Chinese experienced a severe crisis, they quickly abandoned their earlier approach—of reorganizations and exhortations—and employed three principal policies aimed at increasing agricultural production.

To begin with, the Chinese leadership decided to allocate a much larger share of current capital inputs to the agricultural sector than had previously been the case, recognizing this was a necessary condition for increased output. This resulted in much greater fertilizer application and water control in the early 1960s. The leaders not only imported large quantities of fertilizer but also invested in fertilizer plants and in plants producing capital goods for agriculture. In other words, agriculture was a priority sector for investment during this period. The Chinese also restored material incentives to the peasant—he was to be paid on the basis of what he produced—and restored decision-making to the lowest-level unit, that of the production team, which was equivalent in size to the former elementary producers' cooperative. These policies have had the results economists would expect: from that time on, agriculture has been on a significant upward trend. From 1963 to 1971, the estimated rate of increase of grain output was 3.1 percent per year, although the yields in the last few years have not been very good because of unfavorable weather conditions.

This average rate of increase, although admittedly unspectacular, has been sufficient to obtain for the Chinese the agricultural output required to support their military industrial programs. And they have also been able, with the aid of some imported foodstuffs, to maintain a decent standard of living for the Chinese peasant.

More important, not only has output exhibited an upward trend in the last decade but the probability that the rate of growth will be even higher is quite good. The necessary technology is known and the Chinese are proceeding to adopt it, especially increased water control and increased use of chemical fertilizers. While the Chinese still have a long way to go before they achieve the level of inputs that are used in Japan and Taiwan, they are on their way; and those inputs have a proven record of increasing output. Furthermore, there is no secret involved in the solution. The necessary increases in output can be obtained as long as the Chinese are willing to invest their money and efforts, and they are presently doing just that.

Once the Chinese have some control over water supplies and have achieved a high level of use of chemical fertilizers, they can begin to experiment with the new seeds, which have an even higher rate of return. The Chinese have given every indication that they desire to adopt new seeds where possible, and they have sent teams to Pakistan to seek out and work with the new seeds. They also are undertaking their own research in this area. Thus, I believe that the prognosis for increasing the numerator of the ratio of output to labor in China is very optimistic.

What about the denominator in the ratio, which is determined largely by the rate of population growth? First of all, the absolute size of the population must be taken as given. Furthermore, a large population is required in China to maintain current levels of output, given the labor-intensive production techniques used in agriculture. Because the Chinese use such techniques, according to the studies available for the 1930s and the 1940s, and the studies available from China today, there is a labor shortage at the peak seasons of planting and harvesting.

One of the explanations for the failure of the Great Leap in 1958 is claimed to be the attempt to draw off from agriculture large number of people and put them to work in industrial activity, creating a shortage of agricultural labor and forcing those remaining in agriculture to work about 14 hours a day. Thus, it is argued that the Chinese people and land were exhausted at the end of 1958.

Therefore, the size of the population must be considered as an economic benefit. Furthermore, most development economists would argue that it is best to have a surplus population when you launch a large-scale industrialization program, rather than a fully employed population. The latter would mean having to move people out of a sector in which they were already productive and into industry. In China the natural rate of increase in the urban areas is sufficient to fill employment opportunities in industry, and it is not necessary to transfer people out of agriculture for that purpose. Actually, the Chinese are attempting to go the other way: moving people back into the rural areas to avoid the many problems of urbanization that accompany industrialization. In addition to the normal advantage of a "surplus" population, the age structure of China's population is very favorable for economic development. China's population is very young, with the increase in the rate of population growth after the Civil War now entering the labor force, so that the bulk of the Chinese population is in the productive or labor-force ages. This is much different from the situation found in the age pyramids of populations in the mature industrialized countries.

Nonetheless, some control over the rate of increase in population would be desirable; but, as in the case of increasing the rate of growth of the numerator (agricultural output), I believe that the technology for reducing the rate of growth of the denominator is also known. Thus, China does not have to engage in any substantial research on population control because population control techniques are known and discussed throughout the world. What is required is an effective campaign to implement these means of population control, and it would seem that such a program has been launched.

There is no law that says you cannot get married until you are 25; but there exists an effective social standard to this effect, and Chinese youth are expected to abide by it. If they do marry before that age, there is a great amount of social pressure that can be put upon them against displaying antisocial behavior. All of the demographers I have read claim later marriages to be a very effective way to stem the rate of population increase. In addition, intrauterine devices are produced and made available in China. Abortions also are available, but they are not sponsored very strongly because of the lack of trained physicians. Rather, male sterilization is available and encouraged. Finally, ration coupons are said to be hard to come by after the fourth child, or in some cases the third.

Given this tremendous social pressure and official effort, it is my view that if any country is going to succeed in obtaining a reduction in the rate of population growth, China certainly has a good chance of doing so. Most observers believe that population growth in China is on its way down from a rate of 2 percent toward 1 percent; it is probably about 1.7 percent at the present time. Although that still means 1.3 billion people at the end of the century, I have made a rough calculation that shows that, with known technology and the land in China, and if the necessary inputs are made available, the country could support a population of 2 billion without much trouble. Assuming a rapid rate of technological progress, this potential could even increase over time.

My basic argument concerning the agricultural output–population ratio is simple. I believe the recent trend in the ratio is favorable. The possibilities open to the Chinese are even more favorable; and given rational policies in their handling of the problems of economic development this particular ratio should move in a direction that would provide a very good record for their efforts in the next 10 years. But the Chinese planners, of course, are not just interested in an increase in the rate of agricultural output or a reduction in the rate of population.

What is equally important to them is how much of this growing agricultural output can be saved and transferred to other sectors of the economy for investment. The Communist economic system has been specifically developed so as to assure a very high level of savings. The Chinese Communists have implemented many of these methods, such as the transfer of the profits of state enterprises to the state and the use of "forced" deliveries to the state (really purchases at below market prices for agricultural output) to achieve a very high level of savings.

A major problem still exists, however, in that these goods are agricultural goods; and the Chinese have to convert them into capital. In any industrially developed country, these goods can be used to support a labor force that produces industrial capital; but the Chinese labor force was not able, in the 1950s at least (and still is not completely able), to produce its own capital goods. These necessary goods had to be imported in exchange for the saved agricultural goods. This rapid process of capital accumulation was made possible in the 1950s by help from the Soviet Union, which supplied massive amounts of capital.

In the 1960s the Chinese tried to evolve a sort of three-level capital-accumulation program. First, there were the very small-scale, native factories spread throughout the rural areas. The Chinese experimented with these small plants in the Great Leap Forward, but they did not work out very well. They were terribly inefficient and wasteful, inasmuch as the Chinese lacked the necessary techniques in the countryside to really utilize small-scale units to produce high-quality output.

The small-scale plants now being sponsored in the rural areas are more rational, for they apparently are receiving the worn-out or obsolete equipment discarded by modern industries. Local workers are being trained by workers from the modern sector. These small-scale plants, which receive a great deal of publicity, are not responsible for a large share of China's total employment. Nor, despite reports in the Chinese press, can they be said to account for a dominant share of modern industrial output. Yet they are a significant part of China's attack on the development problem and utilize otherwise unemployed resources.

A second-level assault on the technological front is the gradual spread of small-scale, modern factories. For instance, the Chinese are receiving a good deal of assistance from Japan for small-scale chemical fertilizer plants. These are not large industrial complexes but have modern equipment and probably are run by the provincial authorities.

Third, the core of the Chinese industrialization program remains the large-scale, modern industrial plants with capital-intensive equipment. Despite all of the claims made for small-scale industrial activity, if one looks at the trade statistics, if one tours China, or if one reads the popular propaganda, it is these large-scale plants that the Chinese are relying on to develop their own capabilities to manufacture industrial producers' goods. As a result of these efforts to industrialize, a significant rate of growth has been realized. From 1949 to 1971, China achieved an 11 percent rate of growth in the industrial sector. From 1952 to 1971—after recovery from the Revolution—the rate of growth in the industrial sector was about 8.5 percent.

How are we to judge the Chinese performance? I would conclude that despite a very uneven record, including a major agricultural crisis and the Cultural Revolution, during which many people in the West thought China was going mad, the record is fairly good. Simon Kuznets, the recent Nobel Prize winner in economics, in a study of 50 underdeveloped countries, concluded that, on the average, these countries have probably achieved a rate of growth of a little over 2 percent a year in the past couple of decades, after adjustments are made for incorrect prices and statistical biases. In Asia as a whole, that record is even worse.

While I do not desire to present the many different estimates that have been made for China's rate of growth and do not intend to argue for any particular rate of growth, a publication by the Joint Economic Committee (May 1973) that presents the estimates of government experts on China says that the Chinese accomplished about a 4 percent rate of growth since the early 1950s. The report also argues that Western specialists on China who make such estimates err in two directions: first, when things go badly in China, they fail to understand the Chinese leaders' resilience in adopting effective programs to correct a bad situation; second, they become overly optimistic concerning the present good economic results, and talk as if all of China's problems are disappearing. The summary of the report certainly is exceedingly optimistic:

> The People's Republic of China has become an economically strong, unified nation. Its capabilities simultaneously to meet requirements of feeding its population, modernizing its military forces, and expanding its civilian economic base must now be assumed from its record to date. Moreover, its expanding economy and military establishment provided a base for projecting increasing power in consonance with its enormous human resources.
>   Chinese influence may also be felt through both direct use of economic and military aid and in the indirect example of its model of development. Thus, China may in the next decade or two join the United States, the Soviet Union, Japan, and the Western European community in the pentagon of world powers.

I am afraid that the author of that report forgot his own advice not to be too optimistic in a time of good results. Nonetheless, I think that this argument sets a tone much more consistent with the facts than a similar report submitted to the Joint Economic Committee five years earlier. That earlier report provided strong support for what I would call the pessimists in the field of Chinese economics, those who thought that China was on the horns of a dilemma and about to come to a dire end.

I have never been very comfortable in operating with numbers to determine how successful the Chinese have been in their efforts to achieve economic development. Rather, in my own study of China since the early 1960s, I have reached the conclusion that it is the qualitative aspects of China's economic development program that are most significant. Social scientists have been increasingly aware that their quantitative measures of material goods production have failed in their attempt to describe and predict a society's view of its own well-being. Massive and well-financed research projects are now under way with the specific purpose of selecting a better cluster of variables to measure a person's well-being. What matters is not his well-being itself—which is what we thought we could measure quantitatively—but his satisfaction with his actual and changing lot in life. Whatever results are obtained in these studies, I am certain the new qualitative variables will involve such measures as national pride, public health, security, education, equity, and stability.

I do not wish to argue that China's record since 1950 would score well in each of these dimensions. I only wish to point out that the Chinese have allocated more resources and devoted more energies to the problems of modernization than any other underdeveloped country I have read about. Thus an attempt to evaluate their success or failure must involve more than a reference to growth rates for material production.

6

**THE INTERNAL
ECONOMIC SITUATION
IN CHINA AND
ITS IMPLICATIONS
FOR U.S. TRADE**
by Wilford H. Welch

Any evaluation of the probable composition and volume of future Chinese trade with the United States must take account of certain fundamental attitudes of the Chinese and developments within the economy of the People's Republic.

First, the fact that the People's Republic of China is a centrally planned economy, in which trade is not an independent activity, as it is in a free-enterprise economy such as that of the United States, has a direct effect on the conduct of its foreign trade. There is a direct link between national economic planning and the level and composition of foreign trade, both functions being carried out by the government. Imports are determined by the needs of the economic plan, and exports are designed primarily to earn the foreign exchange necessary to purchase the imports. Foreign products that bear no relationship to China's immediate import plans do not represent short-term U.S. export opportunities. Conversely, potential U.S. markets for Chinese goods that do not conform to Chinese production plans do not represent short-term U.S. import opportunities.

Second, the course of Chinese industrial development and China's import plans are influenced substantially by the desire to attain self-dependency. Although the Chinese recognize that in many areas they may not be able to achieve self-sufficiency, they are determined not to be dependent upon the rest of the world for products they consider critical in achieving desired levels of economic or military growth. A corollary of this is a desire to avoid dependence upon any one nation.

Mr. Welch has major responsibility for the Asian operations of Arthur D. Little, Inc. He was formerly special assistant for Asian economic affairs in the U.S. Department of State.

Behind this drive for self-dependency lies the feeling that for many centuries China has been subjected to foreign domination of many aspects of its political, economic, and military affairs.

The future direction of China's economy and trade is also likely to be affected by a third fundamental factor, the desire for balanced industrial and agricultural growth. The Chinese seem to have concluded from bitter experience since the early 1950s that concentration on the industrial sector at the expense of the agricultural sector, or inadequate integration of both, may create more problems than it solves.

The total value of China's imports in recent years from all sources has been approximately $2.5 billion. The figure is quite modest for an economy with a GNP of approximately $100 billion. By way of comparison, Taiwan's yearly imports are currently more than $2 billion per year even though its GNP is approximately $7 billion. It should also be noted, however, that 2.5 percent certainly understates the importance of the role that imports play in the development of the economy of the People's Republic, for it is primarily through the importation of machinery and other sophisticated products that industrial technology is transferred to China. This is in contrast with most developing economies, where technology transfer occurs in large measure through foreign investment and foreign technical assistance. Its need for technology is undoubtedly one of the reasons why 70-80 percent of China's imports are now from the more advanced Western nations and Japan rather than the less advanced socialist countries. It is surely also one of the reasons why the Chinese are interested in establishing trade relations with the United States.

I would like to make some general comments with regard to specific market opportunities for U.S. products as well as the U.S. competitive position. Since 1959, capital and intermediate goods for use directly and indirectly in the development of both industry and agriculture have had high priority in China's import plans. Partly because of foreign exchange limitations, the Chinese have not imported many consumer goods, except wheat and similar basic commodities required to supplement domestic production, in order to feed a population now estimated at 800-850 million.

For the foreseeable future, it seems likely that capital and intermediate goods will continue to represent between a third and half of China's yearly imports. The value of machinery imports seems to fluctuate, not because of changes in import requirements but because of last-minute diversion of foreign exchange to pay for grain imports when inadequate production levels are achieved.

I would anticipate that imports of wheat and other basic agricultural commodities will constitute at least 15-20 percent of total imports over the next few years. This offers U.S. producers a good opportunity despite substantial competition from Canada and Australia.

Military goods, once supplied in significant amounts by the Soviet Union, are for obvious reasons unlikely to be furnished by foreigners in the future. Although the U.S. government's definition of what goods are considered "military" is being relaxed, many highly sophisticated U.S. products of potential interest to the Chinese will certainly be barred from export to China for the foreseeable future.

Given the huge supply of labor in China, many of the labor-saving devices that have been developed in the United States in recent years are not likely to be of interest to the Chinese.

U.S. businessmen are somewhat at a disadvantage with regard to competing for the China market because U.S. export controls and related regulations have totally precluded any economic intercourse between the two countries since the early 1950s. During that same period most of our major competitors in international trade were gradually relaxing their restrictions on trade with China. As a result, the Japanese in particular are well established in the trade. Not only do the Japanese produce many of the chemicals, machinery, steel products, and other goods undoubtedly high on China's import lists, but they have proved to be strong competitors to the United States in most of these products. The Japanese also have a transport cost advantage because of their proximity to China. In addition, the fact that thousands of Japanese businessmen have participated over the past decade or so in the substantial trade that now exists between the two countries gives the Japanese businessman much greater familiarity with the Chinese marketplace and trading procedures.

As if these advantages were not sufficient, it should be also noted that the close working relationship between Japanese business and the Japanese government with regard to the promotion of foreign trade gives the Japanese businessman a strong competitive position. Although increasing U.S. balance-of-payments problems and the changing U.S. government attitudes toward relations with the People's Republic will undoubtedly remove many of the obstacles that have confronted U.S. businessmen in the past, the U.S. government is unlikely to go to the lengths that the Japanese government seems willing to go to assist Japanese business. Many U.S. businessmen cannot help but be discouraged by the array of complicated and frustrating U.S. export control procedures that still affect exports to China. Until recently, U.S. export procedures regarding trade with the Soviet Union, which were not as substantial as those regarding exports to China, still kept U.S. exports to a meager $250 million per year.

Fortunately, there is a brighter side to the bleak picture painted above. The recent devaluations of the dollar relative to the yen will undoubtedly increase the U.S. competitive position in sales to the People's Republic. In addition, the substantial market share that the Japanese have already achieved, nearly 40 percent, undoubtedly concerns the Chinese, who wish to avoid too much dependence upon one source of supply.

The Chinese are likely, under these circumstances, to turn to comparable U.S. products. They are also likely to buy certain U.S. goods because of their high regard for U.S. technology.

In sum, I believe that the People's Republic represents a new market on which a number of U.S. firms should be able to capitalize despite substantial competition from the Japanese and other nations. Success will go to those whose products are highly competitive, who have done their homework, who have determined that they are selling products that are in line with China's import requirements, and who patiently but aggressively pursue these market opportunities.

7

HAZARDS OF PREDICTING
CHINESE DEMANDS
FOR FOREIGN GOODS
by Graham Metson

The leading pragmatic questions that need to be answered in the new era of U.S.-China relations are how to assess the possibilities of trade with China from the standpoint of the American businessman, and how to determine how U.S. products fit into the Chinese scheme of things. In general, I tend to be pessimistic on the possibility of making valid economic forecasts with respect to the People's Republic. I think that its economy is one of the more interesting organizations in the world. It is unique, in fact. But the pricing system is not a major tool of economic decision-making, and there is a determined lack of interest in maximizing economic output. The Chinese do want output, and emphasize this all the time; but they do not want it at the cost of other objectives. The main concern of China is creating the new Chinese man and, in respect to this purpose, even economic output is definitely in second place. The Chinese are very interested in moral and social values and in creating a new morality and a new man.

When you cannot understand what someone is doing, you have to believe what he says he is doing. This does not mean that the Chinese cannot or will not engage in economic analysis. I have talked with planners of other countries, in particular with officials of a country that was a recipient of aid from China. I asked him how the Chinese approached the question of what projects would be most feasible for his country. He was quite frank. He said, "Well, the Chinese approach economic aid very much like your A.I.D. economists do. They compute cost-benefit ratios and all that; they are very tough technical

Trade officer for the People's Republic of China, Bureau of East Asian and Pacific Affairs, U.S. State Department.

analysts. But in their own country, this type of analysis seems to
take second place to the need to create a new man or a new way of
doing things. They find this more moral and more appropriate to the
human situation than traditional capitalist or Communist economics."
Among the books I have examined relating to this point is a very interesting and amusing one, from my point of view. It is Predictions of
Communist Economic Performance, edited by P. J. D. Wiles (New
York: Cambridge University Press, 1971), the conclusions of which
are very similar to my own: that you really cannot tell how the Chinese economy is going to run because of the tremendous political input. Predicting the political future is the essential question in China.
One can go back to charting past developments and on that basis extrapolate a growth rate of, say, 5, 6, or 7 percent, depending on how the
estimates are computed. But there are no solid macroeconomic factors
that one can really analyze. One can try approaching the subject from
the financial side, or from the input side, but one winds up beating a
bowl of taffy—everything pulls together and then separates as you
struggle with it. This does not mean that it is impossible to make
an analysis or to chart a strategy for trade with China. It does mean
that analysis must be conducted in a way different from that to which
we are accustomed. In the case of China, we are dealing with relative
magnitudes.

One can attempt to estimate where he thinks the Chinese are
going to go in the future. One can build a model à la Japan and can
say that China is following Japan in its developmental process. But
when you do this, you have to use very many cautionary qualifications.
In the first place, China does not intend to become another Japan.
The Chinese have no interest in imitating this intensively capitalist
country in any way. I was struck particularly by the fact that Doak
Barnett and I seem to arrive at similar conclusions as to what the
Chinese are going through. (See Chapter 3.) What impresses one
again and again is the autarkic intent of the Chinese, the absolute
refusal at the present time to consider long-term financing, even
though lack of such financing may well thwart the nation's potential
development.

The Chinese apparently are not interested in trade per se. The
allocation of resources in China is very much directed toward an increase of Chinese technology, an increase of the nation's ability to
exist on its own. This has led the Chinese to pursue a somewhat un-
balanced development, from our point of view. They diverge from
our point of view rather sharply in respect to the priorities they pursue.
Sometimes it would seem that the Chinese really know what they are
doing, and then, in the next few years, they move in a direction that
to us appears irrational. They have accepted the premise that
agriculture is the primary source of their livelihood, but they place

great emphasis on industry as well. Consequently they are faced with a rather narrow range of choices in their allocation of resources. Their exportable surplus is only about $2 billion a year, and that amount must serve both sectors. They have chosen to use up to 30 percent of these resources on agricultural imports, chiefly wheat and fertilizer. They use the rest of the money for goods that are partially associated with agriculture, such as trucks and railway equipment.

Directly connected with agriculture are chemical fertilizers and wheat. Wheat imports are important because the Chinese are short of grain. They are actually self-sufficient in wheat, but they use wheat imports to relieve the the pressures on the transportation system. Wheat is imported into the port cities of Shanghai and the North generally, and is used as a substitute for rice that would have to be brought from the South. There is also a certain amount of import substitution. The Chinese can bring in wheat and export a certain amount of rice—which brings in a great deal more money than wheat does. The big factor here seems again to be relief of the transportation system and the improvement of distribution.

It is also worth noting that the Chinese are emphasizing the improvement of transportation and communications in general. These fields appear to be receiving major priority as far as the allocation of resources is concerned. Moreover, for the past few years the Chinese have been paying an extraordinary amount of attention to various types of communication. This concern ranges from aircraft to telecommunications but includes a large number of trucks imported annually, a considerable increase in the domestic production of motor vehicles, and improvement of both railroads and highways. The accomplishments in respect to the transportation systems are remarkable. The Chinese have engineered some of the most difficult rail lines in the world and seem to be making significant progress in terms of local economic development.

Aside from agriculture and transportation, the Chinese are trying to develop a diverse industrial society. Instead of concentrating industry in the coastal cities, the traditional form of development, they have tried to spread their industry out. In many cases they have taken plants that we would consider useless and outmoded and have moved them to provincial cities, sometimes very far inland. This is, of course, related to the Chinese view on how labor should be used. And their view of how to use labor reflects on the moral structure of society. At the same time they have established plants in the interior of China that often are very sophisticated. China's strategic vulnerability undoubtedly plays a role in these decisions. The Chinese seem to be trying to create autonomous industrial units as insurance against possible invasion and the spread of guerrilla warfare. Presumably a decentralized and flexible industrial base is considered appropriate in the context of a military struggle. All these factors are clearly primary inputs to Chinese economic planning.

What does the foreign businessman do with these broad generalities? He begins by making some assumptions about what the Chinese plan is. They certainly want the most advanced technology, and it must be useful to them. For instance, the Boeing 707 is not the most advanced plane in the world, but it is a very useful plane and meets their requirements. They know this. Others have flown it into China for several years; they trust it and apparently it fills the bill. The same is true of the type of telecommunications equipment the Chinese are interested in or appear to be interested in. Sometimes they want equipment so advanced that it is impossible to grant the license to use it. But at other times they seek merely very good equipment and are willing to pay a very good price for it.

One thing I find striking in dealing with the Chinese is that they analyze things very carefully from the cost point of view, but are willing to pay top prices for top-grade goods. One must observe what the Chinese appear to be doing in the marketplace and extrapolate from that what their requirements are. We know, for instance, that for approximately three years the Chinese have been to every conceivable source inquiring about aircraft. We found this out because we would get frantic calls from aircraft brokers wanting to know if we would license aircraft or not, and what kinds of aircraft we would license. We found a general pattern that indicated very strongly that the Chinese are determined to expand their airline system, both internationally and domestically. In effect, they made a major market study in their own fashion: asking everyone possible how much it costs to operate aircraft, how much it costs to buy new aircraft, what can be done with old aircraft, and so forth. I know a number of Americans who were asked in great detail about the American banking system, and each time the question was posed by the same man. He professed complete ignorance about national banks, state banks, the Federal Reserve, what the interplay was, and how the monetary system worked. Each American came away convinced that he was the only person who was interrogated by this particular vice-president of the Bank of China.

No one can predict what the Chinese are actually going to do. But a businessman who is, for example, in communications or telecommunications equipment will learn through his industry sources that the Chinese are asking very detailed questions about various types of equipment. It can reasonably be assumed that they plan some major expansion of their telecommunications network in the not-too-distant future. The same kind of strategy is evident in the case of oil. We have had various predictions as to what the Chinese are going to do about oil. If you start from the beginning, you learn that the Chinese have been importing thousands of trucks at great expense. This is a great drain on their total supply of foreign exchange. They have also expanded their internal automotive facilities, to the point where they claim to have an automotive plant in each province. Some of these plants are nothing more than garages that repair cars and presumably could assemble them from scratch. They probably have a production of five trucks per year. We know the Chinese have decided they want a certain type of distribution system and transportation system. We know that this will require a certain type of fuel. We also know that the Chinese aim, in their autarkic way, to avoid dependence upon outside supply, which means that they are going to have to expand their own sources.

What they are going to expand to is anyone's guess. There is some evidence that they may wish to export oil for a while. My own feeling is that they won't, at least not in the near future. But I agree entirely that they intend to expand their oil industry. From the foreign businessman's point of view, this means that if you are in the refinery products line, you may have a market there.

There is yet another dimension of this subject. The Chinese are asking about various types of oil-well equipment. They have been doing this for some time, but it seems the number of instances has increased markedly. This is probably a signal that they are going to make a major move in the development of domestic oil reserves. I am sure that there will be offshore drilling, though I do not think they will be carrying out operations of any great depth. If I were in the oil refinery business, I would be hustling to make sure I got in on the ground floor.

In conclusion, the macroeconomic factors are almost useless in making predictions as to what one should do with China trade. We know, or assume, that the Chinese economy is going to grow at 5 or 7 percent, or whatever. We assume that more resources will be devoted to international trade, and we hope that some of these resources will be directed to the areas in which U.S. businessmen have a significant interest. But to go further than that in making predictions would be risky.

CHAPTER

8

IDEOLOGY:
THE ULTIMATE CONSTRAINT
ON CHINA TRADE
by Barry M. Richman

The subject of this chapter is ideology in China as it relates to trade, management, and development. Doak Barnett has talked about several of the problem areas in China that could restrict trade—for instance, the leadership problem, which really revolves largely around ideology. The leadership problem in China results from the differing views of what ideology should be in practice, and from the need to arrive at a consensus on this. Barnett referred to the need for a workable relationship between the military and the civilian leadership of the country. This is related to leadership in the broader sense and is again an ideological problem, involving the need for decisions on how far to compromise. He commented on Chinese development; and the underlying fact of Chinese development is that development strategy has been, and will continue to be, in significant measure ideological. Again, whether the Chinese become more moderate or move to extremes, and how far and how fast they try to develop the pure Communist man, will depend on ideology in practice. Even foreign economic policy, including the decision to accept or reject long-term credits, depends largely on ideology because it depends on whether the leadership feels stable enough to assume the risk of long-term commitments. The entire program for economic growth is in large part a function of the leadership's ideological preferences, and of course trade is involved directly in economic growth.

It is clear that China has had a very impressive economic performance to its credit since the Communists took over in 1949, but the record has been very erratic. In some years production has grown

Professor of management and international business, Graduate School of Management, University of California at Los Angeles.

by 25 to 30 percent and in some years it has fallen by 25 or 30 percent. And this record can be closely correlated to the direction in which the Chinese have pushed the ideological pendulum. Where ideological extremism has dominated, economic performance has suffered and management and technical training have dropped off significantly. On the other hand, where the Communists have been relatively moderate in pursuit of ideology, economic performance has been impressive and training has increased quite sharply. What, then, are the important ideological issues and what do I mean by ideological extremism?

Ideological extremism involves pushing ideology in practice beyond the point of managerial or technical or economic rationality. In other words, a decision to let the economy even fall apart for ideological reasons and, in the process, to ignore growth and efficiency, is based on a trade-off calculation between how fast the leaders want social change and the development of a new type of Communist man, and how fast they want the economy to grow. Maoism indubitably contains some very positive factors in respect to Chinese development; it is a question of stopping short of the point of economic and managerial chaos. Mao and his supporters want a nation of pure Communist men, selfless individuals who respond to altruistic and social motives rather than material incentives and self-interest. They want a society that is egalitarian, with few or no class distinctions. Many wish to abolish distinctions between leaders and followers, manual and mental labor, bosses and employees. This is really what they are striving for. In the extreme phase, there are attempts to achieve these objectives virtually overnight, including the abolition of wage differentials and requirements that managers perform physical labor for 50 percent of the time while workers make technical and managerial decisions.

The first dimension of this problem has to do with how much stress is placed on material incentives and self-interest as motivating forces. The second relates to the class struggle, and to how fast and how far class and other hierarchical distinctions can be eliminated. The third part of the problem concerns the role of the militant Reds versus managerial and technical experts. If the decision is to move quickly to eliminate class distinctions, reliance is placed on the Reds, be they the Red Guards or the regular Communist Party cadres. The fourth issue is how much time is spent in political education and ideological indoctrination, both on and off the job. For if a nation of pure Communism is to be attained quickly, you not only need the Reds in charge, you have to make sure of their ideological purity before taking account of their productivity.

I experienced this in reality when I went to China to study the management system. I had previously underestimated the importance of ideology as a motivating force, because I had studied management in Russia, where ideology was a factor but not an overwhelming one.

The Soviets have long stressed material incentives and bonuses and piecework, possibly more than any other country. There are considerable class distinctions in the Soviet Union. It has long been an accepted fact that the experts are to run the economy on a day-to-day basis. The Communist Party sets basic policy and basic objectives, but the detailed planning and controlling functions are essentially accomplished by experts. Distinctions relating to ideology are largely kept out of the workplace.

On the other hand, ideology is a factor of tremendous importance in China and I was there at possibly the best time for undertaking research on it. I was a visitor for a few months before the Cultural Revolution, and again for about a month after it had broken out. As a result I was able to observe, right on the factory floor, the cutting of wage differentials and the stopping of a machine because of the need to give political indoctrination to an engineer who was beginning to think too arrogantly. The important Reds were given jobs that belonged to the experts. But this practice was uneven because it did not have the consensus of the Great Leap Forward. I shall discuss this briefly in an effort to provide a perspective from which one can judge the relative significance of the reduction of material incentives, the elimination of distinctions, political indoctrination on the job, and the substitution of Reds for experts in running the factories and the economy in general.

When the Chinese have not overdone these devices, they have worked very well. When the Communists took over in 1949, there ensued a period of economic rehabilitation from the legacy of idle plants and unemployment of the Chiang Kai-shek regime. There was rampant inflation, so it was not hard to achieve big growth if you stabilized the political leadership and the economy. Industrial output actually grew about 25 percent a year from 1949 to 1952; but this was the effect principally of putting plant and capacity back into operation. A number of private enterprise groups were permitted to continue functioning and were given a period of immunity from nationalization. The Communists did nationalize all private enterprise by 1956, but apparently they are still paying dividends to many of the capitalists from whom they took the enterprises. These were considered the relatively good capitalists and were called the national capitalists. The bureaucratic capitalists associated with Chiang Kai-shek left; if they did not, they would have been in physical danger.

The Chinese regime followed the Soviet development model and the Soviet ideological mode during the first Five-Year Plan, with its increasing stress on material incentives and class distinctions. In general the experts were in charge and heavy industry had very high priority. There was not much stress on balanced growth, but there were some signal accomplishments in agriculture. Centralized ministries were established, and centralized economic management was pursued to the extent that the statistical base made it possible. The economy continued to do well and generated new growth and investment.

Industrial output grew during 1952-57 by about 15 percent a year and GNP grew at an average annual rate of 7-10 percent. This was good growth, but by 1957 or 1958 it was realized that dramatic ideological compromises had been made. Not much time was being spent on political matters; large wage differentials and growing class distinctions were being tolerated, and great stress was being placed on bonuses, piecework, and material incentives. The decision was then made to take the Great Leap Forward, to develop a classless society almost overnight. It was also realized that getting people to respond to altruistic rather than material incentives would generate substantial savings, because even at that time China was still only slightly above the subsistence level. Mao felt that he could get a nation of pure Communism almost overnight, so he put the Reds in charge, hoping that he could both eliminate the material incentives and have high economic growth. The one big difference between the Great Leap and the Cultural Revolution is that the Communist Party generally agreed that the Great Leap, a massive social and ideological program, was worth trying. The Chinese had done well for about eight years. Mao was their hero, and there was little conflict about trying this experiment because they were very optimistic. They were stabilized, they had gotten rid of foreign domination and ownership, and they felt capable of doing anything. There was no sharp party split, nor was there really any significant military involvement. The country went about its experiment, and for a year or two produced grossly exaggerated statistical reports of performance. But by 1960 much of the performance was shown to be mythical.

Eventually the slashing of wage differentials and monetary incentives, the elimination of class distinction, and the other intensive ideological campaigns took their toll, and chaos ensued for the additional reason that nobody knew who was supposed to give orders. Everybody was supposed to be equal, and there were no clear rules of the game. All kinds of industries were established in the countryside but did not work. Mao brought millions of people off the farm and into these industries, so agriculture suffered as well; all of these taken together made the Great Leap a disaster by 1960. Industrial production also started to fall, and between 1960 and 1962 industrial output declined by roughly 40 percent. The GNP fell about 20-25 percent as the Great Leap Forward ran out of control and became an economic rout. It was then that a big wave of emigration to Hong Kong took place. Trade dropped dramatically from the $4 billion peak reached in the late 1950s. In 1961 the Russians—in large part for ideological reasons—called back 22,000 technicians, together with all their drawings and blueprints, almost overnight. On top of that, there was bad weather, which greatly aggravated the agricultural problem. But the economic disaster was, in the end, chiefly of ideological origin. If it were not for ideological extremism, China could have developed its agriculture to the degree necessary to cope with the bad weather of that year.

By 1962 it was evident that a change was imperative. The experts were reinstated, and there was a reversion to a fairly moderate course. However, it should be pointed out that a "moderate course" in China remains more consonant with their ideology than is the case in the Soviet Union. For instance, we are talking about wage differentials of two or three to one in a "moderate" period in China, and one often of ten or fifteen to one in Russia. The Chinese are much closer to their ideology, and it is clear that much of Maoism was highly beneficial up to a point. That is, you can get more out of people if you can get them to strive for psychic satisfaction, social satisfaction, higher needs. Inducing managers to work, say, half a day a week at physical labor is good for communication, because Chinese managers have traditionally had great disdain for physical labor. Mao brought higher achievement drive, higher aspiration levels, and greater dignity. In summary, the 1962-66 period, which ended with the outbreak of the Cultural Revolution, was one of rehabilitation and new growth, and the beginning of a stress on balanced growth, including increased emphasis on agriculture and consumer goods.

After the Soviets pulled out of China (they accounted for most of China's foreign trade in the 1950s), the Chinese started to turn to the West; and within four or five years, 80 percent of the trade was with capitalist countries, very few of which recognized China at that time. The economy resumed its growth from 1962 to mid-1966, and both ideological moderation and trade increased significantly. Indeed, trade reached a new peak in China in 1966, when I attended the Canton Fair. This was in the transition period leading to the outbreak of the Cultural Revolution. Wage differentials were increasing, new elites were forming, hierarchies were arising, bureaucrats were acquiring vested interests in their activities. But this time it was different. There were a lot of people high up in the party who felt that there was a risk of economic disaster in Mao's new line, and they did not want to go that route again. They believed they had learned from history; and they stressed that while they were certainly Communists, they also believed in a gradual approach to Utopia. Their point was that the richer the nation became, the easier it would be to dispense with material incentives and class distinctions. While they still wanted a pure Communist society, they wanted it to come about gradually. Mao apparently became anxious because of his age and what was going on in the other Communist countries. Thus a Communist Party struggle ensued that became known as the Cultural Revolution. However, the process by which the Revolution was accomplished—for example, the directives to engage in self-sufficiency, to cut differentials, to cut bonuses—was unevenly carried out. The new directives were carried out in some of the plants I visited but not in others. It often depended on who was the Communist Party boss at the municipal level, whether the plant was under the municipal authorities, who was Communist Party boss at the provincial level, or who was head at the ministerial central level.

It was this unevenness of response that led essentially to the formation of the Red Guards. They were the most heavily indoctrinated of the young students or peasants, all of them born after 1949. Mao felt that if the Red Guards were sent to the farms and factories to mobilize the workers and peasants, the latter would join together and develop reliable leadership. But the workers and the peasants fought the Red Guards. They liked things the way they were. They did not want to go to extremes. They were reasonably content and the Red Guards, in fact, never took over many factories. But there was a fair amount of violence between August 1966, when the Red Guards were formed, and when they were officially called off in 1968. There was violence, verging at times on civil war, until, by mid-1968, the army began to take firmer control of matters. But by then industrial output had fallen about 15 percent. As ideology declined and military power restored order (by 1971 Mao was sufficiently worried about a military take-over to take defensive action against it), the economy entered a phase of steady growth, beginning in 1969, that has lasted to the present. Industrial growth was about 10 to 15 percent a year and GNP growth 8 to 9 percent a year, which is quite good for China. During this period the military functioned as emergency experts rather than as an entrepreneurial class and was able to bring order out of chaos, and since 1971 the Communist Party seems to be back in power. There are still wage differentials and class distinctions. Political indoctrination on the job and in the schools has been cut back.

Today the experts seem to be running many things under the guidance of revolutionary committees; but it is really hard to detect nationwide patterns, such as could be found before the outbreak of the Cultural Revolution. There is a different ideological climate now. There are the older, hard-core Chou En-lais—allies from a long time ago—some military types, and some Communist Party people, but this is a thinly based and essentially a precarious type of coalition. I think Chou can maintain stability and, as I said earlier, I am optimistic about trade if ideological moderation continues.

Chinese industrial strategy, in the end, really depends on Chinese ideology. How much do they want to trade economic growth for ideological purity? Personally, I believe the Chinese are not going to go through another major ideological upheaval. And if they do not, then trade prospects look very good. There are some signs that they would be willing to accept long-term credits, based on an optimistic assessment of their own leadership and political stability. In 1970 China ran a significant trade deficit, whereas for the preceding 10 years or so they always had a small one. They intentionally did so to build up their industry very fast in key areas, as an offset to losses incurred in the Cultural Revolution. This action showed that they were willing to take a risk. It is probable that as soon as they have the ideological problem solved, they will be willing to take the risks of long-term credits.

If I were to make any predictions, they would be that the trade potential of China generally is anywhere from good to excellent in the next two to ten years, if ideological moderation is maintained. Trade prospects will turn sour if there is ideological extremism, and there will be foreign policy problems as well. If ideological extremism threatens to produce a civil war (as in the case of the Cultural Revolution), Chinese leaders might feel impelled to create an external threat (perhaps the Soviet Union) as their last resort to unify the country. And that could be the biggest foreign policy danger. Should there be any reversion to the Red Guard mentality, trade and much else are likely to suffer.

In their day the Red Guards would indoctrinate you for two or three hours before they would talk business. They would make you sit on the floor and would read to you from their Chairman Mao books. I think one must be alert to any symptoms of recidivism in this regard. Happenings of this sort, including the schools closing again or the militant Reds reassuming a commanding role, are the best indicators for predicting what the Chinese are going to do in terms of economic performance and trade. To the extent that developments of the kind mentioned appear remote, and assuming that we do not begin hearing again about new revolutions actually being implemented to eliminate wage differentials, class distinctions, and the like, the situation is likely to continue to be relatively calm and stable. If we begin again to hear about a new Cultural Revolution or a new socialist education campaign, that could very well be a danger signal. But I don't think the Chinese are going to go to the extreme in the forseeable future. I think they are going to settle for a trade-off of somewhat improved economic growth together with a reasonable degree of ideological purity, rather than try to maximize growth. I do not expect economic performance at the Japanese level, but I do think China can maintain an industrial growth rate of 10 to 12 percent per year and GNP growth of around 6 to 8 percent a year, and that is a very respectable rate of growth.

THE POLITICAL
AND ECONOMIC
FUTURE OF TAIWAN
by Yuan-li Wu

The political and economic future of Taiwan will affect first of all the Republic of China and the lives of the residents of Taiwan. What that future should be is, therefore, a matter for them to decide; their choice and their effort will by and large determine what that future will be. I propose to outline some of the choices available and to discuss some of the conditions that may affect the practical range and viability of their choices.

To say that Taiwan can choose its own future is not merely to affirm one's faith in free will or to make an empty gesture against historical determinism. There are at least two good reasons why Taiwan's future is very much in its own hands. First, what Taiwan chooses to do will be a factor shaping the international environment within which the island's future will evolve. The policies of other nations toward Taiwan cannot help but be influenced by Taiwan's policies; the more one does for oneself, the more likely will one be to receive sympathy and aid from others. This is, of course, one of the tenets of the Nixon Doctrine, and in practice it may govern the conduct of other nations that have an interest in the Western Pacific. Second, Taiwan is able to make its own choice because what would otherwise be a most potent source of threat to its freedom to do so is especially constrained in the present international context. I mean by this that the People's Republic of China, which has continued to insist on the "liberation" of the island, is today neither in a military position to assert its will nor in a political situation vis-à-vis both the Soviet

---

Professor of economics, University of San Francisco, and consultant, Hoover Institution on War, Revolution and Peace, Stanford University.

Union and the rest of the world, especially the United States, to use force in the Taiwan Strait. Fear of the Soviet Union, which is realistically based on the presence north of its border of 1 million Soviet troops, equipped with the most sophisticated weapons, and the perception of a possible Soviet preemptive strike against China's burgeoning nuclear force, has persuaded the People's Republic to seek rapprochement with Washington and to present an image of reasonableness and of a nonaggressive, inward-looking attitude, while its arms buildup continues.

In the circumstances, it would behoove Peking not to seek a solution of the Taiwan problem by force. In the Shanghai joint communiqué, Chou En-lai declared that he would not subscribe to the use of force in solving international disputes. While he continues to insist that Taiwan is a province of China and that therefore its status is an internal issue, Chou has in effect acquiesced to U.S. military presence in Taiwan until stability in the region, a somewhat undefined geographical area, is considered by Washington to warrant the total withdrawal of U.S. forces. Chou has thus tacitly agreed not to use force to challenge the U.S. presence in Taiwan or the repeated U.S. assurances that it will honor its treaty commitment to the Republic of China. In addition, it would not be easy for the Chinese Communist forces to achieve air and naval supremacy for an invasion of the island; and without such supremacy it would be difficult to secure superiority on the ground. Thus the entrance of Peking into the United Nations and the U.S.-China meetings in Peking have led to an open admission (1) that there are issues more important to Peking than the "liberation of Taiwan" and (2) that the Chinese Communist forces are not in any military or political position to be used against Taiwan. Consequently the military threat to Taiwan, long quiescent, has, if anything, receded further rather than increased. This implies that the people in Taiwan will not be prevented by military force from making their own decisions.

The nature of the choices available is always a function of the outlook of those making the choices. If we apply this general principle to the political future of Taiwan, we can theoretically distinguish among the following categories of persons and what they consider viable options:

1. Those who are sentimentally attached to the concept of "one China," including Taiwan, and who care not whether this China will be Communist or non-Communist, would regard eventual reincorporation of the island with the mainland as a viable alternative.

2. Those who want "one China," a non-Communist one, may look forward to eventual reincorporation if they believe that the People's Republic is once again moving toward revisionism and that this time the end will be the abandonment of Communism, not just Maoism, as an ideology.

3. Those who do not believe that Mainland China's leaders have really discarded their Communist mantle and/or who believe that Taiwan should seek an independent role in the comity of nations, separate from Mainland China, would reject incorporation with a Communist-controlled mainland as a viable option. Some of them would advocate an independent Taiwan, whatever may happen on the mainland. Others would seek a postponement of the issue for future decision. Some of those who hope for delay do so on the ground that after Mao Tse-tung and/or Chou En-lai passes from the scene, the People's Republic may cease to function with an effective central seat of power and that the Communist threat, a major reason for Taiwan to make a conscious choice, would then disappear. Others hope for delay because they are still weighing the pros and cons of the alternatives.

In addition to the above, there are some intermediate groups. For instance, there are those who would prefer to see an independent Taiwan but who find that the "one China" concept has the merit of neatness in terms of international politics. Consequently, they would favor autonomy for Taiwan within a one-China framework. This, they argue, might be accomplished through bilateral negotiations.

Let us now consider which of the above alternatives seems to be acceptable to the people on Taiwan. In the first place, it should be noted that bilateral negotiations between the authorities on Taiwan and in Peking have already been emphatically ruled out by the government of the Republic of China. The reasons for this attitude are several. Some Nationalist Chinese leaders believe that the Chinese Communist leaders have not changed, that the seemingly more moderate attitude exhibited by Peking is a stratagem designed to win time for Peking's Soviet-oriented deterrent policy and to weaken Western support for Taiwan. These Nationalists maintain that it would be futile to seek a peaceful solution of the "one China" issue by negotiation. Furthermore, they are against negotiation under duress, which would be the situation if they were to negotiate following the admission of Peking into the United Nations. This attitude of non-reincorporation into a Communist-controlled mainland and of non-negotiation is shared by those Nationalists who are anti-Communists and those residents of Taiwan of whatever origin who can find no strong attraction to seek a return to the mainland. In fact, for most of the present residents of Taiwan such a "return" could at best be only a sentimental journey with neither economic nor political appeal.

For those Taiwan Independence Movement members who see little support in the new international environment for an independent Taiwan without the cooperation of the erstwhile "mainlanders," the best chance for Taiwan to remain an independent entity seems to lie in working with the Republic of China authorities. It is equally clear to those authorities that their best defense against mainland political warfare is to reinforce internal political cohesion by increasing representation and participation of the local population in government. If Taiwan has thus ruled out its eventual incorporation with the mainland if the latter is controlled by the Communists, the remaining options call for Taiwan to stay as a separate entity, whether or not such an entity will eventually become a separate state. Retention of both options requires the same set of political and economic preconditions: the promotion of greater political cohesion and increasing economic well-being for the island's population. It is significant that the government and the people of the Republic of China have for the past three years vigorousl[y] pursued policies that have precisely these objectives. It is also impor[-] tant to realize that these are policies that redound to the benefit of the population and should therefore be pursued because of their intrinsic merit.

As a result of changes in the special provisions governing the period of "national emergency," the National Assembly voted in March 1972 to give the president of the Republic of China discretionary power[s] to expand representation of the "free areas" in the electoral bodies of the central government. The number of native Taiwanese repre- sentatives has since been increased by 36 (8 from professional groups and 28 on the basis of residence) in the Legislative Yuan and by 10 in the Control Yuan. Compared with the original number of members of these two bodies as of 1972—425 in the Legislative Yuan and 66 in the Control Yuan—the above increments for Taiwan are 8.4 percent and 15.1 percent, respectively. In addition, the 20-member new cabi- net formed by Chiang Ching-kuo has 6 members who are of local origin. The cabinet posts involved include deputy prime minister, minister of communications—a vital post for an island nation—and minister of the interior, plus three ministerial posts without portfolios[.] Since both the new governor of Taiwan and the new mayor of Taipei are also of local origin, Taiwanese representation in the higher eche- lons of the executive branch of the government is far from negligible. Of perhaps even greater import than these changes is the fact that a precedent has been set to give an increasing voice to the residents of Taiwan. This will lend greater meaning to whatever political choice they may eventually make.

While the internal political changes noted above are relatively recent and therefore probably less generally appreciated, the impres- sive record of Taiwan's economic development is familiar to most of us. Only a brief description of some of the background data will, therefore, be necessary. In this connection I would like to draw atten- tion especially to some recent trends and certain benchmark years.

First, 1962 seemed to be a benchmark year. Before then, Tai- wan's gross domestic product (GDP) grew at an annual rate of 5 to 7.5 percent, having fallen from a high of 12.9 percent in 1951-52, the peak of the post-World War II recovery period. After 1962 the growth rate has been around 10-11 percent a year.

Second, making the above GDP growth rate possible was a series of significant increases in the rate of capital formation. The ratio of gross capital formation to GDP rose to 20 percent in 1959-60 and to over 25 percent after 1965, when U.S. economic assistance was ended.

Third, gross domestic savings rose from 60 percent of gross domestic capital formation in 1960 to over 80 percent in 1963. Since 1965 it has been around 90 percent, with foreign credit and capital accounting for about 10 percent.

Finally, between 1964 and 1970, imports rose by 272 percent while real national income rose by 61 percent. The growth of imports, some financed by foreign credit, was matched by an increase of 233 percent in exports. The economy has become more export-oriented and more import-reliant.

The developments noted above imply that as an island economy, Taiwan has based its rapid development upon the expansion of imported materials and equipment and that this expansion has made possible the accelerated growth of exports. This is how the process sustains itself. With this expansion of overall trade, the economy of Taiwan has succeeded in achieving a rate of growth of output, together with a high ratio of capital formation sustaining this growth, that clearly points to further economic expansion and a breaking of the shackles of underdevelopment. The economy has also been able to finance capital formation with domestic savings, so that it no longer has to depend upon foreign aid for the financing and support of further development. What foreign imports, partly financed by foreign investors, now provide are essentially (1) technology that is embodied in some of the imported equipment and materials and (2) a part of the expanding export market that foreign investors bring with them when they make goods for export. The expansion of Taiwan's three export-processing zones exemplifies the second function most clearly.

All this is to say that Taiwan is now in a position to continue economic growth as long as its export and import trade can expand without interruption, and as long as foreign investments can continue to flow into the island. It has already chalked up a good record of such growth. The various benchmark years I have cited indicate that the successful economic transformation of Taiwan on a sustained basis has lasted more than a decade if we measure from 1962, or eight years if we measure from 1965, when U.S. economic aid was phased out. In the absence of some powerful adverse influences, this trend is unlikely to reverse itself.

Following its U.N. defeat in October 1971, the Republic of China embarked upon a program of expanding international trade and investment, especially with the European Economic Community, Latin

America, the Caribbean, the South Pacific, and Africa. Diplomatic relations are no longer considered a sine qua non of economic intercourse. As a matter of fact, trade with a number of countries, such as Italy and Belgium, has increased considerably despite their switch of diplomatic recognition to Peking.

In the foreign investment area, a joint investment project in a major steel complex has been initiated in cooperation with Austria, a country that has recognized Peking. Discussions are currently under way between Taiwan and European banking interests regarding a loan for the electrification of Taiwan's railway system. Above all, U.S. investments have continued to expand in Taiwan and the volume of credit and guarantees by the Export-Import Bank has grown. A recent statement by that bank will not escape the attention of other foreign investors, because it anticipates the expansion of U.S. credits. Investors who are becoming increasingly interested in Taiwan may find the island a suitable place for producing exports to Asian and other markets because of the low labor costs and the competitive advantage it confers. One may recall in this connection the large flow of U.S. investments to the Common Market that were attracted to the benefits of expansion there. By the same token, U.S. and European capital may find it advantageous to invest in low-labor-cost countries such as Taiwan and South Korea, in order to compete with and in Japan, as well as in the larger markets of the Pacific Basin and the world.

Only in the case of Japan was there some initial hesitation after October 1971 about making new investments in Taiwan. Some Japanese businessmen seem to have become extremely sensitive to Chou Enlai's "four principles," according to which China would deny its business to those Japanese firms that deal with South Korea and/or Taiwan or have investments in either country. However, even in this respect Peking seems to have been quite practical. According to reports from Japan, some Japanese firms that have accepted the "four principles" have nevertheless been denied more trade with Peking because their prices rose too high after revaluation of the yen. On the other hand, Japanese firms that have declined to recognize the "four principles" have nevertheless been able to expand trade with Peking because their products happen to be in demand and are suitably priced. On the basis of past experience, one would assume that Japanese business will be able to find means of continuing to trade with both Taiwan and Peking.

Taiwan is now prepared to trade with all "non-hostile" countries, including Communist ones, although the initial mode of operation may take the form of indirect trade via third countries. This, of course, is the extreme example of all recent measures that have had the effect of countering the efforts by Peking to isolate Taiwan internationally. These measures have in fact had the positive effect of significantly expanding Taiwan's external trade.

The agrarian reform of Taiwan has largely benefited the former tenant farmers, who were almost exclusively of local origin. The more recent expansion of other economic sectors has led to the rise of many Taiwanese capitalist and business interests. Thus far the economic benefits have probably accrued more to the residents of local origin than to the more recent immigrants. There are also reports that the income spread between the rich and the poor in Taiwan has declined during recent years and that it is far narrower than the range in other Asian countries. If the authorities and the population in Taiwan can further reduce these income differences while raising the absolute level of income, and if the usual disparity between the cities and the countryside can be further lessened, the strength of the middle class will increase and the Republic of China will have built a strong bulwark against external threats in the next generation. If we assume that Taiwan can continue its vigorous economic growth and that the benefits of economic expansion will be shared by all segments of the island's population, one could well raise the question of why residents of Taiwan would wish to opt for reincorporation into a Communist-controlled mainland. Even though the political future of the island has not yet been determined, it is at least clear what the choice will not be.

10

CHINESE PRIORITIES
AND THE PROSPECTS
FOR U.S.-CHINA TRADE
by Barry M. Richman

There is no question that China desires to build up its trade and its trade potential rapidly. A major constraint that could emerge is another shift toward ideological extremism, a subject with which I have dealt in Chapter 8.* If the country, and those who are in charge of it, want to move quickly again to attempt to develop a nation of pure Communist men in the Maoist mold, in which there are virtually no class distinctions and very little emphasis on material gain and self-interest, in which Reds or super-Reds or Party ideologues, rather than experts, will be running industries and individual enterprises, and in which great amounts of time will be spent in political education and indoctrination, then the whole economy will probably slump significantly. In such circumstances chaos may erupt, as it did in the Cultural Revolution and in the Great Leap Forward.

Such a movement would sharply temper any optimistic judgment on trade prospects I might make, because it will interfere with imports and exports, foreign policy, and everything else. My assessments are, in consequence, based on the assumption that ideology in China does not go into an extreme phase again.

China is today at the stage of relative self-sufficiency in agriculture and in other sectors, to the point where it can think seriously about, and develop the delivery system to become, a first-rate industrial power quite quickly. China is not going to depend indefinitely on Japan as such a major source of supply. There is little trade with Russia. The Chinese will want to follow a diversified trade strategy with major

---

Professor of management and international business, Graduate School of Management, University of California at Los Angeles.

*See also B. Richman, Industrial Society in Communist China (New York: Vintage Books, 1972).

countries. And since they're starting from a low base with the United States there's a good chance for rapid growth of that trade even in the short run.

The best indicators of China's trade potential, by markets, is their current Five-Year Plan, which began in 1971 and ends in 1975. Some data are available, and I have also acquired some data informally from Chinese officials in various countries. Their industrial strategy is tantamount to a kind of technological revolution, involving the rapid building of complete plants, which necessitates the purchasing in the short run of large-scale machinery, equipment, and, in many cases, know-how. Prior to the Cultural Revolution, there were more than 22 companies putting up complete plants—companies from Japan, Western Europe, and other parts of the world. Some of these contracts involved many thousands, even millions, of dollars; but contract performance was interrupted by the outbreak of the Cultural Revolution. However, these undertakings have a history going back only as far as 1973. It is now possible to enter into agreements with the Chinese involving the payment of service fees, and even licensing. At this stage I think the Chinese would be willing to try virtually anything except equity ownership.

Consider the fourth Five-Year Plan. Primary emphasis is on agricultural plants and equipment. The Chinese want to build up a mechanized agricultural capacity very quickly, by means of tractors, fertilizers, and the like. Then comes mining equipment, which is a very big field because China is rich in mineral resources. Oil, coal, metals and minerals, and the chemical and construction sectors have very high priority and are likely to have strong influence on imports by the Chinese. Motor vehicles of various kinds, machine tools, oxygen generators, air compressors, and assorted motors, pumps, and bearings are also items in which they want to be self-sufficient in the not-too-distant future. It is in manufacturing (apart from aircraft and communications, where reliance may be placed primarily on imports) that one finds the sectors in which the Chinese want to build up their own technology. It follows that aircraft and communications are the sectors in which the greatest import opportunities lie in the near future.

How are the Chinese going to pay for their imports? It appears certain that they will be making use of long-term credit because of their desire to develop the full capacity of their known mineral resources, which requires a heavy investment in equipment and technology. The lead time needed to accomplish such a project is substantial. That means that the Chinese are not going to utilize only short-term credits. They have sufficient bargaining power to seek longer credit terms, including their past integrity in business, their adherence to financial obligations and contractual agreements, and their evolving worldwide reputation. So there is a pretty good chance that they will get larger and longer terms.

The Chinese are going to step up their exports considerably in raw materials (as these are more intensively exploited), agricultural products (especially the more exotic foodstuffs that would appeal to affluent societies), and a wide range of consumer goods: textiles, arts and crafts, sporting goods, toys, furniture, rugs, and cashmere sweaters. There is an almost endless list of relatively labor-intensive items that they can produce well and competitively, a trend that over time could parallel the Japanese evolution in foreign trade.

The Chinese are now almost ready. They have gone through textiles, batteries, and similar items and are probably at the transistor stage now. I think that in a few years we may see China exporting transistorized radios, television sets, and other types of electronic components that are relatively labor-intensive. I think the Japanese realize this, and that is why they are moving into much more advanced technology. The Chinese will respond by stepping up exports very quickly, but there is going to be a gap that will have to be filled with credits if they are to accomplish what they want to do in this fourth Five-Year Plan and beyond.

Politics has not really entered into trade relations between China and Japan. It probably will not enter into U.S.-China trade, unless the ideological element becomes extreme again. From what I have been able to find out, the Chinese may continue to make political decisions that occasionally conflict with economic rationality in trading with small countries, mainly the less-developed ones. For example, they stopped buying cotton from Egypt several years ago as a kind of political reprisal and switched their patronage to Pakistan and Tanzania. The Chinese are more likely to trade for political reasons with less developed countries than with major countries; for instance, they will sell, far below cost, things that they are inefficient in producing, such as equipment and machinery, to less-developed countries. But it is unlikely that they will sell very much below cost, or even below a reasonable profit margin, to major countries. An exception might be an item requiring two to three years to build up the volume and efficiency needed to yield larger profit margins.

The Chinese are quite pragmatic in foreign trade and have a different kind of pricing system for foreign markets than for the domestic market. Most of the prices of major commodities are fixed by the state as part of the state plan. The market does not have much significance in China itself, although in general there has been more response to market needs in China than in the Soviet Union. In any case, firms in China that are major exporters operate with different bookkeeping systems. In particular, they often receive various subsidies on the materials allocated to them. Thus, they can usually maintain their customary profit margin on export orders, even though they sell at less than the domestic factory price.

One thing that impressed me, having spent most of my time with producing firms rather than in trade negotiations, is the pervasiveness of the priority of exports among producers, even though the managers of producing firms rarely negotiate with foreign businessmen. Such negotiation is conducted mainly by state trading corporation officials and foreign trade officials. Even though foreign businessmen have very little contact with the actual producers of Chinese exports and the actual users of imports, there would appear to be a strong concern with exports harking back to the export emphasis of the mid-1960s. Thus, even if a substantial supply bottleneck exists (very prominent in planned economies of the Communist type), export orders will typically take priority. If an export order comes in suddenly, operations will be disrupted to meet it on time.

Another very interesting thing is the large percentage of people engaged in quality control for export-oriented firms. In many such firms 10 percent of the total personnel is concerned with quality control. If they don't have much expertise, they just add manpower and multiply the levels of inspection. There is much evidence, in short, of a commitment to exports and an awareness of their importance. The Chinese do sell some things below cost in foreign markets—for instance, in less-developed countries—and they may adopt the same procedure in more advanced countries in the short run. Of the many companies I visited, only a few were selling their products below cost, for instance, in Hong Kong. The items in question included fans and batteries. However, more traditional goods—textiles, cashmere sweaters, and arts and crafts—were selling significantly above cost, though still a little less than the retail consumer price in China.

There are many examples of this practice, and they have been commented upon by others. Together they provide some idea of Chinese pricing strategies from the inside, of the way they do their bookkeeping, and of the behind-the-scenes role that the producers play in foreign trade. The fact that China is a planned economy and that there is no capitalist-type market mechanism should not, in my opinion, be of great concern to people in foreign trade, given the high priority of foreign trade throughout the economy. Foreign trade has until very recently been stressed much more in China than in the Soviet Union. I have studied industry in the Soviet Union, and there has been less stress on quality control there than in China, although I assume that most Russian exports are of reasonable quality.

I have found that it is generally easier to negotiate with the Chinese than with the Russians. They are hard bargainers, but they generally seem to do more homework and often to have more discretion and authority for spontaneous decision-making further down the line.

The decisions do not appear to have to go through nearly as many committees in China, unless a huge order like the Boeing 707 deal is involved. A typical order, anywhere up to a few million dollars, will not usually have as many bottlenecks and other obstacles as might be thought, once the negotiating starts. There is also generally not very much leeway for price-cutting. The Chinese are pretty competitive in their prices, although they do make some concessions. They have built up loyalty to major customers and suppliers from other countries. And while it is believed by some that you can go in and steal these markets en masse, so long as you have a little better price, this is simply not true.

The real U.S.-China trade potential, I think, is with the new things that the Chinese are going to produce—the new kinds of technology they need, on the export side, from the United States. They are building up a significant and growing supply capacity in respect to exports to the United States. They have many items that could prove most attractive to American consumers and that are geared to an affluent society. Chinese exports to the United States generally should not bother U.S. labor unions very much, because many of China's major exports will not have an effect on unemployment or on displacement of labor in the United States. All in all, and keeping in mind the ideological pendulum I mentioned, I am quite optimistic about trade between China and the United States over, say, the next two to five years and beyond.

11

U.S. OPPORTUNITIES
IN THE CHINA MARKET
by Wilford H. Welch

I would like to discuss the present U.S. competitive position concerning exports to the People's Republic of China and the specific product areas where we at Arthur D. Little believe the major U.S. export opportunities lie. To successfully take advantage of the market opportunities that theoretically exist, U.S. businessmen must be aware of and must overcome several adverse factors.

First, U.S. firms are latecomers with no experience in dealing with the People's Republic, whereas most of our competitors have been in the trade for a number of years. I emphasize this because experience has shown that the Chinese prefer to deal with those who have made the effort over the years to establish a relationship of mutual trust. Unless a product is something that they have a unique desire for, such as a Boeing 707, it is likely to take most U.S. firms sometime before they are able to effectively inform the Chinese of their products and establish the type of business relationship needed to maximize trade potential.

Second, many of America's most competitive products are not likely to be the subjects of contracts in the near future. Undoubtedly, America's greatest competitive strength now lies in the production of highly sophisticated technological goods and in the service industries. Many of our high-technology products are not, however, likely to enter the trade either because of continued U.S. export regulations concerning goods perceived to have military value to the People's

---

Mr. Welch is with Arthur D. Little, Inc., of Cambridge, Massachusetts, where he has major responsibilities for the firm's Asian affairs. He was formerly special assistant for Asian economic affairs in the U.S. Department of State.

Republic, or because of China's inability to effectively utilize such items. With regard to services, the People's Republic has shown itself reluctant to allow foreigners to establish themselves in the country for extended periods of time or to become directly involved in China's industrial or trade development.

Third, with the exception of agricultural commodities, many of the goods that the United States produces, and for which there is a Chinese demand, are also produced by the Japanese. The Japanese not only have proved to be strong competitors to the United States in general but have a transport cost advantage in export to China. In addition, Japanese business already has established relations with the People's Republic and has the benefit of more active support of their government in pursuing new opportunities.

Fourth, China and most of our competitors use the metric system.

Fifth, although U.S. export controls with regard to sales to the People's Republic are in the process of substantial liberalization, these controls are likely to remain more extensive than those of our major competitors.

Although most of the negative factors cited above should be the cause of much concern and underlie the need for adjustment in many aspects of U.S. business and trade policies, there are a number of countervailing factors that strengthen our competitive position.

First, the fact that subsidiaries of U.S. firms are located throughout the world puts us in a unique position. The book value of total U.S. investments abroad is more than $75 billion, or 60 percent of total foreign investment, which is valued at $125 billion. As a result, U.S. subsidiaries, whether in Japan, Singapore, Hong Kong, or elsewhere, are often in a strong competitive position to sell to the Chinese even if the parent company is not.

Second, it has become evident that the Chinese think highly of U.S. technology and are anxious to acquire it when it is relevant to their needs.

Third, the Chinese are anxious to diversify their existing sources of imports and to expand trade as well as other ties with the United States. This desire is, of course, rooted in political as well as economic factors. Specifically, the Chinese wish to avoid overdependence upon any one supplier, such as the Japanese, for critical imports. Since the Japanese now supply nearly 40 percent of all of China's imports, there are already indications that the Chinese are prepared to pay a premium to avoid much more dependence upon Japan. Since Japan is our major competitor for the Chinese market, this encourages the Chinese to look to U.S. products wherever feasible.

Fourth, the devaluations of the U.S. dollar relative to the Japanese yen will undoubtedly help the U.S. competitive position versus the Japanese.

Fifth, the increasing flexibility shown by the U.S. government to solve the balance of trade and balance of payments problems and to reduce obstacles that have prevented U.S. exports to China in the past has been an essential first step. It is likely that further steps will be taken that will not only reduce obstacles but will also actively support sales.

I would like to turn now to potential market opportunities for specific U.S. products or categories of products. In recent years China's chemical imports have been valued at more than $200 million per year, or between 15 and 20 percent of all imports. Approximately half of all chemical imports have come from Japan.

Manufactured fertilizers, primarily nitrogenous ones, have constituted nearly 50 percent of all chemical imports. Although the Chinese have a substantial domestic fertilizer industry, their plants are for the most part small and do not supply the country's total requirements. As a result China is the world's largest importer of fertilizers.

It is our view that the sharply increasing cost of feeder stocks, principally natural gas, in the United States will make it difficult for the United States to produce fertilizers that can compete with the Japanese products for the China market. One exception might be exports of nitrogenous fertilizer from production facilities located on the southern coast of Alaska. Another is exports from subsidiaries based abroad. A more likely U.S. opportunity appears to be the sale of whole fertilizer plants and U.S. production technology relating particularly to large-scale ammonia fertilizer plants.

With regard to organic chemicals, such as the intermediate substances used in manufacturing plastics, pesticides, and pigments, Japanese plants are for the most part newer and more efficient than U.S. plants. This factor, coupled with lower transport costs, makes the Japanese strong competitors.

It is difficult to generalize about the competitive position of the United States in the Chinese inorganic chemicals market because many diverse products with different cost characteristics are involved. The Chinese do have many basic raw materials to be developed, however, and opportunities certainly exist for the export of U.S. plants or plant technology.

Agricultural products, particularly wheat, represent approximately 20 percent of total Chinese imports and are valued at more than $200 million. The extraordinary size of the Chinese population is suggested by the fact that such substantial wheat imports represent less than 5 percent of China's total wheat requirements. Wheat certainly represents a major trade opportunity, although strong competition will continue to come from Canada, Australia, and France. Changes in U.S. regulations concerning trade with Communist countries certainly enhance U.S. wheat export prospects.

As for potential export opportunities for forest products and related equipment, it should first be noted that the per capita consumption of paper and paperboard in China is among the lowest in the world. For example, in 1970 per capita consumption in China was approximately 11 pounds per capita, compared with 554 pounds in the United States. China's forest resources are, however, a modest one-seventh of that of North America, which suggests that certain products will have to be imported. A recent study conducted by Arthur D. Little, Inc., indicates that U.S. producers are in a strong position to supply China with pulping, papermaking, and paper- and board-converting equipment, as well as a number of forest products, such as pulp, newsprint, and liner board.

Major opportunities appear to exist for U.S. producers of manufacturing equipment and whole plants. Chinese interest will undoubtedly be centered on equipment and plants incorporating much of the high technology developed in the United States. Among the types of U.S. machinery that may prove attractive to the Chinese and in which we are in a relatively strong competitive position are internal combustion and diesel engines, agricultural machinery and tractors, precision instrumentation for control of manufacturing, food-processing machinery, sophisticated machine tools, plastic- and rubber-working machinery, and supplies for the mechanical industries, such as ball, needle, and roller bearings and cutting tools for lathes and milling machines.

Although Chinese imports of construction equipment have been modest because of reliance on their own substantial labor supply, China may import heavy-duty and specialized construction machinery because of its quality. Sophisticated U.S. mining machinery, including that used for the exploration of their oil, coal, and other mineral reserves, is likely to be of particular interest.

With regard to U.S. transport equipment, the market potential for passenger and cargo aircraft, trucks, buses, locomotive, and related equipment appears substantial. A problem here may lie, however, not in the Chinese interest in such items or in our competitive position but, rather, in the willingness of the U.S. government to approve sales of products considered to have military value.

Although the Chinese market for iron and steel products has been and is likely to continue to be sizable, the strong Japanese competitive position with regard to most iron and steel products may limit direct U.S. exports to specialty steels.

The discussion thus far has focused entirely on the potential Chinese market for U.S. commodities and has taken little note of the potential for the U.S. service industries. With time it is likely that U.S. banks will establish relations with the People's Republic despite the current reluctance of the Chinese to have them do so. I would anticipate that U.S. shipping will also benefit from expanding trade relations, as will U.S. airlines.

In sum, I would like to emphasize that even though the emergence of trade relations between the United States and the People's Republic of China represents only a modest market opportunity for the United States as a whole, it appears to offer a number of extremely attractive opportunities for a select number of U.S. firms and their foreign-based subsidiaries.

12

CHINA'S FOREIGN TRADE
POLICIES AND PRACTICES
by Kenneth D. Gott

China's foreign trade is not only a state monopoly but also a highly centralized one, and this immediately brings out one practical point for those wanting to conduct trade with China. That point is that no one is likely, in my opinion, to be able to conduct any trade with the People's Republic outside China or Hong Kong. There is no opportunity at present, nor do I think there will be in the future, to conclude trade deals with Chinese embassies or Chinese trade attachés stationed at embassies abroad. The fundamental point is that the trade policy of the People's Republic is very strongly influenced by political considerations. This fact has practical implications for the near-term evolution of U.S.-China trade.

On economic grounds there are good reasons to believe that China might, in the near future, take advantage of the lifting of the trade embargo by President Nixon to purchase technologically advanced U.S. products. However, there are some obstacles to be considered.

The question of sequestered assets on the part of both countries needs clarification. Not least in importance, of course, is the determination of the future status of Taiwan. Next there is the Chinese policy of self-reliance, which influences all of their decision-making. Indeed, the virtual obsession with self-sufficiency would appear to leave a rather marginal role for foreign trade. This is reflected in the figures, which show that foreign trade, both ways, represents about 4 percent of the Chinese GNP, imports and exports each representing about 2 percent. These are very small figures by world standards.

Managing director, Business International Asia/Pacific, Hong Kong; former editor, Business International, New York.

A further point I would like to develop is that the Chinese are not, at present, interested in taking foreign credits or loans. They are very proud of the fact that, in keeping with their principle of self-reliance, the government has no internal or external debt. Shortly after the foundation of the Communist regime, some government bonds were floated for internal financial purposes. These bonds have since been retired. There was a period when the People's Republic had an external debt to the Soviet Union. That debt was repaid by 1965 or 1966, and the Chinese claim that they have no internal or external debt is quite true. I don't think this is the best way to run a shop, least of all a less-developed country like China, but that is the way they prefer it. If I give you a somewhat low-key picture of the prospects of U.S.-China trade, it is based on the assumption that this attitude toward foreign debt will continue.

If the assumption is made that the Chinese will be willing to accept foreign loans and credits, a very different picture emerges. China's credit standing in the world trading community is extremely high, and it would experience no difficulty whatever in obtaining credits from Western Europe and from other sources.

As far as trade with other Communist countries is concerned, the Chinese generally operate with bilateral trade treaties, attempting to balance imports and exports with respect to each Communist trading partner. With regard to less-developed countries, the practice is to barter to some degree and to conclude bilateral trade pacts in other cases. The barter of Ceylonese rubber for Chinese rice is one example of such deals. In dealings with the industrialized nations of Western Europe and Japan, the Chinese conduct their trade on a multilateral basis, that is, much as the United States conducts its foreign trade. There are no special peculiarities in the trade between China and Britain, for instance. Such trade resembles, in essence, trade between Britain and France.

A few words on the composition of Chinese trade are in order. The Chinese import capital goods. They import certain raw materials required to keep their industry running, rubber being an outstanding example. Since 1951 they have had to import some quantities of foodstuffs, particularly wheat from Canada and Australia. Again, as a result of the food situation, they have imported increasing quantities of chemical fertilizer in recent years. But there is no market of significance for consumer goods in China. Foreign exchange is far too scarce to be used on consumer products. Capital goods, raw materials, foodstuffs, and the chemicals associated with agriculture form the bulk of imports.

On the export side, the Chinese are able to supply large quantities of agricultural products, of minerals (manganese, tin, tungsten, mercury), and an array of consumer products. Most of their consumer products are not very good quality by Western standards. They make sewing machines that look somewhat passé. They make a range of light industrial products that, while they find a ready market in the less-developed countries in Asia and increasingly in Africa, are not up to the standards required for marketing in the more sophisticated economies.

Turning for a moment to the structure and organization of Chinese foreign trade, the People's Republic in many ways resembles the Soviet Union. There is a standing committee of the National People's Congress whose authority is exercised by the State Council, the head of which is Premier Chou En-lai. Under the State Council are the various ministries, one of which is the Ministry of Foreign Trade, the key one as far as this discussion is concerned. The economy is directed through a series of Five-Year Plans, the present plan being the fourth, which runs from 1971 to 1975. Exactly what the goals and particular projects under that plan are, have not been made public in any detail.

The Five-Year Plan sets targets and tasks for the various ministries. The ministries that find they need equipment or materials to fulfill their targets fill out commodity volume cards for the goods needed. These are sent to other ministries that may be able to supply the goods and materials needed. If the domestic industry cannot meet the demand, the card will then be referred to the State Planning Commission. In the light of total demand, the Planning Commission decides whether or not the goods are to be imported and notifies the Foreign Trade Ministry. This very capsule description of the procedures is meant to identify the center of the process from the foreign trader's point of view: the Foreign Trade Ministry. It also contains a practical lesson: there is probably a limited realm for salesmanship as far as selling equipment to the People's Republic is concerned.

If the product one is trying to sell is on the import list deriving from the Five-Year Plan (and the inability of the Chinese to produce it), there may be an opportunity to sell it. But if it is not scheduled for import under the Five-Year Plan, one is probably wasting his breath trying to sell it. The Foreign Trade Ministry coordinates not only the country's total demand for imports but also the quantity of goods to be exported in order to pay for those imports. Since China does not accept any sizable quantity of foreign aid, its international reserves, while adequate, are by no means sufficient to withstand a trade deficit for any length of time. It follows that exports and imports are kept in a pretty close balance. That is why, in discussions of China trade, we very often speak of two-way trade. If we are talking about a volume of trade of, let's say, $4 billion a year, it is logical to conceive of this being equally divided between imports and exports, because the two are in approximate balance.

If the trade amounts to $4 billion, then imports will tend to be a little less than $2 billion and exports a little more, because the Chinese operate conservatively and try to get a slight trade surplus each year, usually $200 million or so.

The international reserves of the Chinese, according to estimates of the U.S. State Department, are at present around $820 million. They are sufficient for approximately five and a half months' imports, which is reasonably good in comparison with the situation of such countries as the Philippines and India.

Under the Ministry of Foreign Trade are 10 state import-export corporations: the China National Chemical Import and Export Corporation, the China National Machinery Import and Export Corporation, and others structured along similar lines. There is a corporation for cereals, oils, and foodstuffs; there is one for light industrial products; there is one for metals and minerals; there is one for "native produce" and animal by-products; and there is one for textiles. Finally, there are the trading corporations concerned with shipping, transportation, and books and periodicals. These import-export corporations, the prime targets of firms wanting to introduce their products to the China market, are the organizations that do the actual trade. An important feature of the China trading scene in the case of those foreign companies that have done China business over the years (and I am thinking of British and Swedish companies in particular) is that they very rarely see the end-user. Standing between the foreign seller and the end-user in China are the officials of the import-export corporations. This point will be covered later in regard to efforts some companies have made to bypass the screen of officialdom and get through to the actual users.

Working closely with the Ministry of Foreign Trade is the China Council for Promotion of International Trade. This body tends to move onto the scene when trade exhibitions or trade missions from countries that do not have diplomatic relations with the People's Republic are involved. In other words, when a trade mission or a trade exhibition from a country that has diplomatically recognized China is involved, the Ministry of Foreign Trade will generally be the responsible negotiating party; but in dealing with countries that have not diplomatically recognized China, the China Council for Promotion of International Trade might play host to a trade mission, or something of the sort.

Turning now to some considerations of policy, prewar China trade had been mainly with the United States, Japan, Britain, and other countries of Western Europe. But in the years following the proclamation of the People's Republic, foreign trade was directed very heavily toward the Soviet Union and the Eastern European nations. This was Mao Tse-tung's "policy of leaning to one side." And the years after 1950 saw a very rapid growth in the type and amount of China's foreign trade. Trade grew from about $1.2 billion in 1950 to $4.3 billion in 1959, a peak that was not reached again for some years. Growing friction with the Soviet Union after the death of Stalin, and the sudden withdrawal of Soviet technicians in 1960, caused a contraction of trade that was not made up until 1970.

In the 1950s, something like 70 to 80 percent of China's foreign trade was with the Communist bloc. Since the rupture of relations with the Soviet Union, the direction of China's trade has shifted to the point where today about 70 percent is with the non-Communist countries and only about 3 percent of it was the Soviet Union and Eastern Europe. While the China-Soviet rift was a major factor in the redirection of China's foreign trade, it should also be noted that beginning in 1961, there was a series of bad harvests and other agricultural troubles that brought China into the world market as an importer of wheat and foodstuffs.

It is worth remembering that an important feature in the golden age of Chinese economic growth and expansion of foreign trade in the 1950s had been massive infusions of technical help from the Soviet Union, including construction of many complete plants and industrial complexes. There were, at one stage, some 10,000 Soviet technicians working in China and some 15,000 Chinese students in the Soviet Union. The Soviet Union contracted to build 291 major installations; and by the time relations were broken off, 130 of these projects had been completed at a cost of about $1.3 billion. East European nations had undertaken to supply 100 projects, 66 of which had been completed by 1959, when the rupture in relations came. This aid, some of which was provided on credit terms, enabled China's industry to expand at quite a rapid rate in that period. It also resulted in temporary creation of debt to the Soviet Union, which the Chinese, as indicated above, had completely paid off by about 1965.

After China switched the bulk of its foreign trade to non-Communist countries, the volume of that trade rose fairly slowly until 1966, when it had reached $4.2 billion, almost the level of 1959. Then came the Cultural Revolution in the late 1960s, which again saw a fall in foreign trade. But by 1970 foreign trade was up to $4.2 billion, and 1971 saw trade overtake the 1959 level and set an all-time record of $4.5 billion. It is safe to assume that the trend will continue.

Putting this in perspective, China's foreign trade for 1971 was only slightly ahead of that of Taiwan. There is every indication that, given the faster growth of foreign trade in Taiwan (which is heavily oriented toward foreign trade, while the People's Republic is not), that little island will in the near future cut a bigger figure in world trade than the People's Republic.

If we turn now to some political factors, it is useful to note that China has, in the last few years, had very good trade relations with Indonesia and Cambodia. However, each of those countries underwent a critical change in which a left-wing government was driven from power and a more conservative one replaced it. As a result Chinese trade with these countries shriveled. Understandably, China set out to expand its trade with Cuba when Castro came to power. It set about expanding its trade with Albania when that nation took its side in the dispute with the Soviet Union. More recently China has been showing very favorable interest in trade with Romania, because of Romania's independent stand vis-à-vis the Soviet Union. These are examples of the way politics continues to govern the pattern of Chinese foreign trade. Another, and perhaps more telling, example is the fact that at a time when China was buying its wheat primarily from Australia and Canada, Canada extended diplomatic recognition to China in 1971. However, Australia, after some abortive attempts to engage in a dialogue with Peking after President Nixon's visit, gave up the effort. As a result China has boycotted Australian wheat ever since.

Enough has been said about politics as a big factor in all of the trade policies of the People's Republic, but I think it only fair to note some exceptions. China purchased wheat, wool, steel, and other products from Australia at the time when Australia had troops in Vietnam. It also made purchases from New Zealand at a time when New Zealand troops were in Vietnam. West Germany, China's biggest trading partner in Western Europe, is one of the few European countries that has not recognized the People's Republic. Finally, China's biggest trading partner worldwide is Japan; nevertheless, the Chinese regime was quite hostile on political grounds to the Sato regime, which it described as one of the main enemies of the People's Republic. This was doubtless a significant factor in the subsequent change in the Japanese leadership. Thus, while politics has been a big factor in China's trade policies, one must not exaggerate the point.

Turning now to some of the practices of China trade. An essential part of the foreign trade mechanism of the People's Republic is the Canton Trade Fair, held in the spring and autumn of each year. Originally these twice-a-year fairs were designed to promote Chinese exports, but they have become the major occasions on which Chinese foreign trade deals are concluded. Each of the fairs lasts a month, and it is estimated that 20 to 50 percent of China's total foreign trade is conducted at them. This situation is unique in world commerce. No other nation centralizes so much of its foreign trade into a pair of fairs. Such an arrangement has an obvious advantage from the Chinese point of view. On the one side of the negotiating table there are the officials of the import-export corporation, and on the other side there are the buyers and sellers from dozens of nations competing for business. It creates a supply-and-demand situation that obviously favors the Chinese, whether they are trying to buy or to sell, because they are able to maximize the competition among the foreigners.

Moreover, the trade fair technique minimizes the impact of foreigners on Chinese society. Instead of having foreign businessmen trooping into Shanghai and Peking throughout the year, they are confined to Canton for two months. This is not to say that the foreign trade missions and individual businessmen do not get to Peking. They do, particularly when major deals in wheat, steel, aircraft, and such things are concerned; but the importance of the Canton Trade Fair cannot be overlooked as an adjunct to the machinery of China's foreign trade.

Next, there is Hong Kong, which is a foreign enclave where foreign firms may, in season and out, contact Chinese Communist officials, including bankers and trade officials. Rearing up near the Hilton Hotel is the Bank of China Building, an omnibus center for Chinese government activities. It is a bank. It is probably also the headquarters of the Communist Party. It serves as an artificial consulate; and on its ninth floor it houses an extremely important organization, the China Resources Corporation. This is probably the most important organization in Hong Kong for a would-be China trader to know about. It represents four of the most important of the import-export corporations, those for metals and minerals, machinery, chemicals, and textiles. The import-export corporations for light industrial products and for native produce and animal by-products are represented by another agency in Hong Kong. The cereals corporation is represented by the Ng Fung Hong Company.

Hong Kong thus remains the first point of contact for the increasing number of U.S. companies that have been trying to break into the Chinese market. In our office in Hong Kong, we have had a stream of American businessmen wanting advice on how to go about contacting the Chinese, how to go about getting invited to the Canton Fair, and so forth. Our advice to them in nearly all cases is to make contact with the China Resources Corporation in the Bank of China Building, assuming that their product is one that falls within its jurisdiction. We further advise that there should be no attempt at this stage to talk business deals. Above all, there should be no attempt to quote prices or get into any figure work. American companies should content themselves, at this first point of contact, with making the company known and placing its catalogs and sales literature in front of the Chinese. It is our experience that the Chinese at this point in the negotiations are not yet ready to buy American products.

Invariably, American visitors to the China Resources Corporation in Hong Kong receive a friendly welcome. This is significant, because when I first went to Hong Kong in August 1970, Americans visiting the China Resources Corporation were usually given a lecture on the evils of imperialism and the atrocities being committed in Vietnam by American forces. Recently, however, the atmosphere has completely changed. The Chinese are welcoming Americans in the same spirit in which they put out the red carpet for them at the Canton Fair. They are very receptive to information, particularly technological information, sales catalogs, and things of that sort; but they are not yet ready to sit down and talk about deals.

I would suggest that if you want to prepare for significant U.S.-China trade, you should seek at this stage to put your literature in front of the Chinese and to make your companies known to them, stressing in any covering letters that you merely wish to introduce yourself, and that you are interested in friendship and world peace, and a few generalities of that sort. If you have any relevant addresses, go directly to the import-export corporations in Peking. That will perhaps get you a step farther toward the end-user. But I would not suggest that at this stage you make any efforts to contact ultimate end-users in China. A brief anecdote will illustrate the points being made here.

A certain organization managed to get itself a representative in Peking, an American working as a translator for one of the government publishing houses. We have a number of clients in the pharmaceutical field, and we had inquiries from these companies as to whether we could get them addresses of hospitals, clinics, and medical institutions in the People's Republic, so that they could mail samples and literature directly to these end-users. I asked the American in Peking if he could get me a list of Chinese hospitals; he said he could not, because there is no central source from which he could get such a list. That is the kind of centralized, extremely secretive, society China still is.

However, using our Chinese research staff in Hong Kong over a period of several weeks, we were able to compile from Chinese magazines and newspapers a list of approximately 100 hospitals in China with their addresses: the People's No. 2 Tuberculosis Clinic in Shanghai, the Osteopathic Hospital in Peking, and so forth. We made this list available to those of our clients who wanted to send samples. Some weeks went by, and I was invited to visit one of the "unofficial spokesmen" of the Chinese Communist government in Hong Kong.

This gentleman, call him Percy, was as charming a person as you could wish to meet and was, in fact, the subject of a small article in _Time_ magazine some time back, concerning the role he played as propagandist and front man for Peking. Percy had me in for a talk, in the course of which he berated my company for drawing up the list of hospitals. That was not going through proper channels. He insisted that anybody wanting to get samples or catalogs to China should send them through the China Resources Corporation. The China Resources Corporation would then pass them on to whichever organization in China would have an interest in the material.

He implied that the China Resources Corporation was perfect in its operations; and that no matter how complicated the information, it knew exactly to whom it should go. I was a little skeptical of this but did not say so. His clinching argument was, "Don't attempt to send in literature in this way because we control the post office it goes through."

In short, I suggest that you not try to leap over the curtain of officialdom that stands between you and the end-user in China. The most productive course is to abide by the rules prescribed by the Chinese.

PART

V

DEALING WITH
THE CHINESE

13

NEGOTIATING WITH
THE CHINESE
by David C. Buxbaum

This chapter will focus narrowly on my experiences, or the experiences of my firm, in doing business with China.

We had done a considerable amount of research before we arrived in China. We represented not only ourselves but also several major American corporations and several smaller enterprises, including a major corporation in the transportation field, a small corporation in the field of specialized technology and animal husbandry, and a major corporation in the textile field. It was our good fortune upon arriving in China to find the Chinese very accommodating and sensitive to our wishes. We were able, within a period of 25 days at the Canton Fair and approximately a week in Peking, to consummate 25 agreements and to commence discussions on a number of others. We returned from the Canton Fair and continued to communicate with the Chinese on almost a daily basis. We are presently in communication by cable, by letter, and by other means.

We have found, to our great pleasure, that negotiating with Chinese corporations and responsible Chinese officials has not been nearly as difficult as had been alleged by many people who had been there before us. We have found them to be reasonable, precise, and exacting. They were very interested in our markets, in the corporations we represented, and in the backgrounds of these corporations. They were especially interested in exactly what was going to be done with the product that they were selling and in the exact long-range intentions of the corporation from which they were considering purchasing goods.

There are numerous impediments to trade between China and the United States. Several of the economic impediments have been discussed. There are others that we believe will be transitory,

President, May Lee Import-Export Corporation, New York.

especially in respect to the use of American banks to deal directly with Chinese banks. The Chinese have raised the question of frozen assets, including Chinese assets frozen in the United States. We know, of course, that there is a problem relating to American goods confiscated in China in retaliation for our actions in 1950. We must also be aware of the problem that arises because China does not enjoy most-favored-nation treatment by the United States. The result is that Chinese products are much more expensive in the United States than they would be if China did have most-favored-nation status. This restriction not only inhibits to some extent the purchase of Chinese products by the United States but also inhibits sales to China and, to that extent, raises an appreciable obstacle to the full exploitation of China's trade potential.

There is also the problem of direct shipment to China, which is impeded by Transportation Order No. 2 and other U.S. regulations.* In fairness, it must be said that the Chinese have endeavored to do what was possible in the face of these impediments.

Finally there is the problem—which I hope will soon be solved— in regard to sending parcel post packages to China. Though it is still not possible to send airmail packages from China, parcel post packages can be sent from China to the United States.

This is a very brief synopsis of the various impediments that we have found in trade with China. Let me turn to may own experiences in dealing with China. I am often asked the question, "Should we work through other firms with established relations in China, including the use of experts or consultants?" It is my advice (and this may be self-serving) that one should use experts or consultants or agents to deal, or at least to facilitate one's dealing, with China. First of all, experts, if they are indeed experts, can provide information that is valuable to you. One of the questions asked is, "How do we distinguish the experts from the non-experts?"

If you are dealing with a corporation rather than an individual, you do the normal thing in determining whether or not the corporation is viable. What is the Dun and Bradstreet rating? What are its banking relationships? Is it a substantial corporation? In short, you perform normal business checks.

Finally, with regard to the individuals who are involved in trade— and there are only a handful who are experts in this field—you can certainly check their background, their academic references, their facility in terms of knowledge and language. This information is not secret; in fact, it is fairly easily come by. Some corporations have

---

*American ships are not allowed in Chinese waters and vice versa.

not been astute and cautious in determining who the experts are, and they have acquired a jaundiced view of experts as a result. But the important point is that the question of determining who is an expert and who is not, is really not as mysterious or as difficult as some seem to believe.

Second, a question has been raised as to whether or not it is necessary to use the Chinese language. Should Chinese be used either in negotiations or in the presentation of a proposal to the Chinese? I have been told on numerous occasions that use of the Chinese language is really unnecessary, indeed that it is undesirable. Some corporations have reported that in some instances the Chinese told them they don't want to use Chinese. Well, I find all this very difficult to believe. I am sure that I could not have negotiated the 25 agreements in the short number of days that I was in Canton, Peking, and Shanghai if I did not speak Chinese fluently. I am also certain that we facilitated numerous proposals by presenting them in both English and Chinese. I am sure this has been true not only of our corporation but also of other corporations and other individuals who represent clients in China. The use of English in China is uneven. There are some people and some organizations that are very proficient in English. There are others who have a much more modest level of English. The use of Chinese facilitates transactions in terms of speed and of getting down to points that are essential in consummating a deal. I conclude that the use of the Chinese language is very important.

Furthermore, it is a question of attitude. I believe that in some instances the American executive, given the speed with which he operates, becomes used to a rather capsule way of dealing with people. From a Chinese point of view, at least, this amounts to being impolite in his dealings. The Chinese are, of course, aware of the differences in cultural norms and cultural modes of expression. Nevertheless, I think that in working in any foreign environment, it is very desirable to be attuned to the foreign way of doing things. If one can adapt himself to the Chinese way, he enjoys a distinct advantage, in my opinion.

Most of the Americans who went to China on the most recent trip were quite sensitive to Chinese cultural preferences, even though many of them were not experts. They deliberately and very carefully made an effort to become sensitized. There was one individual who was an exception and behaved almost as a kind of caricature of a "big businessman" in China. The result was that this individual was in one instance very politely asked to leave the meeting in which he was taking part. This is an extreme case. But I do think that sensitivity to the cultural nuances of Chinese methods of doing business is most desirable and most helpful. There again, I think experts can be of assistance.

At the risk of being trite, I recommend that you or your representative be prepared on all facets of your business proposal before you go to China. If you are planning to make a purchase, you should be familiar with the nuances of a Chinese purchase agreement.

A word about contracts. It has been noted that the Chinese occasionally may wish to have certain political material in the contracts. Several of the corporations we represented were concerned about the inclusion of this type of material, which could have posed insuperable obstacles to the consummation of the contract. Fortunately, the question of inclusion of political information or statements never arose; and all contracts were very simple, straightforward documents.

There are other, more customary problems that arise with contracts, such as breach of contract, in which the methods by which and the jurisdictions within which such disputes are resolved must be determined. In this connection it is important to note the precedents in existing Chinese practice and thus what one might anticipate in terms of one's contractual negotiations. In fact, of course, the Chinese are very scrupulous and are almost invariably willing to renegotiate a transaction in which there has been a dispute over performance.

14

COPING WITH
POLITICS AND PEOPLE
IN THE CHINA TRADE:
THE CANADIAN EXPERIENCE
by Pat Clever

I shall try to put the Canada-China experience into perspective with a few illustrative highlights. Canada-China trade really began with the wheat trade. To see the wheat trade in perspective, it must be remembered that, as a country, Canada relies far more heavily on trade than the United States. Whereas U.S. foreign trade is about 5 percent of GNP, Canada's approaches the 33 percent mark. Our total external trade for 1971 was $33.5 billion, almost 70 percent of which was with the United States. An opportunity to trade with others was welcome to us as a means of lessening our reliance on one customer and one supplier.

Wheat is a peculiar commodity in Canada and, I think, to a large extent, in the United States. When one talks about wheat in Canada, he is talking about a politically charged subject—more precisely, the farm vote, of which the government is keenly aware. Long before Canadian recognition of China, the Conservative administration under John Diefenbaker made the first wheat sale to China, with considerable fanfare. At first there were a number of raised eyebrows; but the farmer, it turns out, doesn't really care who gets the wheat as long as he gets the money. So that once people get over the initial shock, they are quite prepared to sell more.

The present administration of Prime Minister Pierre Trudeau was, in effect, elected partly on the assumption that he would begin the steps leading to diplomatic recognition of the People's Republic. From the time he assumed office until negotiations for recognition were concluded, more than two years passed. Some of the goings-on at the Stockholm negotiations were indeed esoteric. The Canadians

President, Canadian Manoir Industries, Ltd., Toronto.

told the Chinese that if they (the Canadians) were to be restricted to a radius of 24 kilometers from Peking, the Chinese would be restricted to a radius of 25 miles from Ottawa. At which the Chinese declared, "Oh, you cannot do that, that is discrimination." The Canadian negotiators said, "Why not? You restrict us, we'll restrict you." The Chinese answered, "Ah, but we restrict everybody and you are only restricting us and therefore it is discriminatory." I am happy to say we stuck to our guns. If they want to travel more than 25 miles from Ottawa, the Chinese must obtain permission.

To get back to the wheat deal. The benefits to Canada from such trade are both political and economic. First, we sell a commodity that is in considerable surplus and in the production of which we compete with the United States, Argentina, France, and Australia.

During my first visit to the People's Republic, I was repeatedly asked, "Why does your government recognize the bandit government of Taiwan?," after which the Chinese stated the thesis that they were doing Canada a great favor by buying wheat they didn't need. Well, if you hear such a statement often enough, you get pretty tired of it, so at the farewell banquet, after a couple of mai tais I decided I was going to issue my challenge. I did this in a very roundabout way, saying, "Well, let's look at this. The Canadian farmer toils very hard and struggles to plow the ground." "Oh yes," they agreed. "Then he sows the wheat, which involves a lot of hard labor." "Oh, yes." "And then the railroad carries it to Vancouver and then ships carry it to the northern ports of China, and you unload, and that is a lot of trouble." They agreed with all of this. And then I said, "This is a lot of trouble just for a favor, so why don't you forget about the wheat and send us the money?" They thought that was rather humorous and tendered a revised explanation of what they had really meant. They said that taking our wheat wasn't only a favor, although of course it had that element in it; it was also useful to China, and this was the recompense for the favor extended. This usage of words may not mean a lot to us, but it does to them. That is their approved vocabulary. They dodge behind it and feel very safe.

The Chinese said the wheat was useful because the world market for rice was extremely good, so much so that one pound of rice could be sold to their friends in Southeast Asia for enough money to buy two pounds of wheat from Canada. The deal was doubly profitable because they gained needed foreign exchange and the people in North China preferred to eat wheat. This adds up to a rather pure form of altruistic exchange between China and Canada, I suppose. There is both political and commercial benefit for both sides. In Canada, domestic pressures favoring wheat exports to China led to recognition. The Canadian recognition of China did not do Canada any harm at the United Nations. It certainly was the beginning for

China of a desired falling into place of a number of things. The availability of wheat imports put China in a position to sell rice in Southeast Asia on favorable terms, which translates into political influence. Since the rice is more expensive and the wheat cheaper, the Chinese gain a hard-currency benefit that they can use to purchase essential imports. At the same time, they can provide profitable foreign aid, as in Peru. In addition, they reap the advantage of being able to give the people in North China a commodity they prefer to rice, creating a feeling of well-being.

It really doesn't matter where the Chinese buy wheat, because now that they have achieved political recognition, the leverage they enjoyed in Canada is equally available in the United States or in Australia. Clearly, trade and politics are very closely linked.

One further practical aspect of the China trade is the kind of people the West should send to China.

The greatest mistake a major company can make is to send a new team to each Canton Fair. Doing that will lead to having absolutely no "face" with the Chinese and no identity for the company. People are important to them. It takes the Chinese a little while to assess those with whom they do business, and this assessment is partly the purpose of the political conversations at the outset. If new people are sent every time, they will not get to know who the company is. My advice would be to pick someone with mature judgment and considerable patience, and to give him as wide a latitude as possible— he should not have to check back continuously. Send him in with a clear-cut frame of reference within which he can most efficiently conduct negotiations. He should expect to devote considerable time to this activity.

Let me tell an anecdote that illustrates all this. The scene is a discussion room in Shanghai in September 1969. I arrived with Mike Gold, who has been in the China trade longer, I believe, than any other Canadian. His commodity is gloves. I was in Shanghai by mistake, forced to wait four days for my visa. One day the Chinese said, "Did you see men land on the moon?" We answered, "yes, we saw it on television." "Could you tell us something about it?" We started telling them about it. Mr. Gold said, "Would you like to see some pictures?" He pulled out the edition of Life magazine that had as its cover a picture of the astronaut standing in front of the flag. The Chinese called others to look at the material. If you could take pictures simply by looking hard at something—well, they were taking pictures. It took them twenty minutes to examine that issue. Then they ceremoniously handed it back. Mr. Gold's discussion leader said in Chinese to the interpreter, "Ah, the Americans are very foolish people. They have paid $500 million for one pound of moon dirt." Mr. Gold leaned over the table, almost to the point of being out of his chair, and with his face about a foot and a half from his negotiation leader, said with a straight face: "You offer identical commodity at better quotation?"

How does China trade? Well, the glib one-word answer is "slowly." It holds a good deal of truth. Any foreigner dealing with China—be he importer or exporter, buyer or seller—is dealing with "city hall." Every person that he comes in contact with—the room boy at the hotel, the ice cream seller in the park, the waiter at the restaurant, the officials at the state trading corporations—is an employee of that super conglomerate, the Chinese state.

In ordinary trading circumstances, we accept certain basic rules. If you purchase substantial quantities of manufactured goods, your personnel deals with representatives of the manufacturer and you have ready access to the factory technical personnel. Your people are able to discuss modifications of product and packaging with people who are familiar with the production process. If you are a seller of goods—and in the Chinese context we can confine ourselves to capital goods and basic commodities—you send a man who is familiar with the technical capabilities of your production facility and he who can recommend modifications to make the equipment as useful as possible. He would expect to deal with the manufacturer who is planning to use the equipment.

In China, neither the seller nor the buyer deals with factory representatives. The line of direct communication between the manufacturer and the buyer, and the manufacturer and the user, is through the state trading corporations. The staffs of these corporations are composed largely of nontechnical administrative personnel.

All imports and exports are handled through the state trading corporations. At one time there were as many as 12, but to the best of my knowledge there are now only seven. The activity of each corporation is preceded by the words "China National" and is followed by the words "Import and Export Corporation." The most current list I have is as follows:

Cereals, Oil, and Foodstuffs
Native Produce and Animal By-products
Textiles
Light Industrial Products
Chemicals
Metals and Minerals
Machinery

With the shortened list of corporations, it is a little easier to guess who handles what; but there still are some anomalies. Leather gloves come under Animal By-products, gloves that use synthetic materials come under Light Industrial Products, and some of the knitted items come under Arts and Crafts, which used to be a separate corporation but is now a department of Light Industrial Products. In essence, one attends the Canton Fair and finds out who carries what.

To go to China in order to discuss business, you must have an invitation from one of these corporations. If you do not have an invitation, you will not be able to obtain a visa. There is a very distinct difference between going to China in connection with the Canton Fair and a visit between fairs. At the fair, time is at a premium; you compete for appointments with others interested in your commodity. Buses take you from your hotel to the fair buildings; and when the attendants take the ropes down, there is a rush to get the appropriate sections first. It is not unusual to make an appointment for the next day or the day after; and if you are interested in only one commodity, you have nothing to do until then. You should have bilingual business cards. Be sure that when making your appointments, the Chinese understand what you are interested in and where you come from.

At the first appointment the process is deceptively informal. If it is your first visit to China, you will be asked about your impressions and will likely be engaged in some political discussions. It appears that the Chinese attempt to get an impression of you before any business commences. Now you are ready to discuss some business. It is advisable not to hurry the process. To the question of what they would like to sell in your country, it is as likely as not that you will get the answer: "What would you like to buy?" A fellow named Kaufman from Montreal swears that he participated in the following discussion at his first visit to the fur section of the Canton Fair:

Do you have any Tibet plates?	No.
Do you have any kolinsky?	No.
Do you have any rabbit?	No.
Do you have any calgans?	No.
Well, what do you have for sale?	What do you want to buy?

Still, one is not left with the impression that these procedures are designed to test one's patience; they appear simply to be the Chinese way of doing business.

Once you have conducted some substantial business with the Chinese at the Canton Fair, enough matters may have accumulated to require a meeting between fairs. A very different atmosphere prevails then. During the fair, the Canton hotels are humming with activity and resemble an international business conference. A regular social life develops, and there are many parties. Between fairs you are likely to stop at the virtually empty Tung Fang Hotel. There is no activity of any kind. If you are traveling to other cities, you will still meet with the Canton branch people while you are there; these meetings are more exhaustive. You are generally picked up at your hotel between 8:30 and 9:30 and the meeting breaks up at noon, when you are taken back to your hotel.

In the afternoon you start between 2:00 and 3:00, the session lasting until approximately 5:00. Hours of meeting in other cities are much the same. In Shanghai you walk to the corporation offices. In Tientsin the discussions take place in your hotel. In Peking you are likely to take a taxi to the office or to be picked up by corporation representatives at the hotel. At meeting you may be confronted by as few as three people, including the interpreter, or as many as nine. The functions of the various people are rarely explained. All negotiations that I have attended have been conducted in English through an interpreter.

Perhaps the most difficult situations are those involving politics. Sooner or later you will be involved in a political discussion; and if you are smart, you will not have started it. Remember that you are talking to a very doctrinaire people and that no matter how logical your argument, you are not likely to convince them of your point of view.

You don't necessarily have to agree with them—you can tell them that in your country their way would not work. My advice is to avoid direct confrontations, as they serve little purpose.

Suppose you have succeeded in negotiating some substantial orders, and have returned to Hong Kong. Payment will be via irrevocable letter of credit; this can be arranged through any number of banks. What are Chinese standards in terms of adherence to price, quality, quantity, and delivery? There will be no change in the price. The quality as a rule is quite reliable. In quantity, you may find underruns or overruns to an extent that you are not accustomed to in dealing with other countries. Substitutions are also a problem. The worst single feature is the unreliability of delivery times. I do not believe that this is done purposely. You must remember that you are dealing with a country that has over 800 million people but has only 25,000 miles of railroad. Long-distance road transportation is still undeveloped. Perhaps the factory had the goods ready but could not get cartons on time. Or all was ready but there was no transport to the port. Or the goods reached the port on time but the limited sailings of approved vessels did not allow your corporation to get the required space.

The shipping season for the East Coast ports in Canada faces a winter interruption; and if the last boat has gone, the merchandise must wait until the next season. This applies particularly to porcelain and earthenware. The bulk and the weight in relation to the value do not permit overland shipment from the West Coast. In general, the conditions described do not allow for the scheduling of goods in the sense that consumer goods are scheduled in the North American distribution system. In purchasing Chinese merchandise, one should allow for profitable disposal at any time that it becomes available, be this six months late or a year late. In that sense, Chinese merchandise is opportunity merchandise and must be priced to allow for these uncertainties.

In many instances there is a shortage of merchandise, so that at the Canton Fair you will find insistence on minimum quantities but refusal of contracts because of the large size of the order. If a contract is refused because of inability to supply the quantity demanded, you are rarely told. You find out by asking if half that quantity might be available. Sometimes the Chinese will accept and confirm; sometimes no confirmation is issued. Shortages are expressed both in pricing and in rationing. The Chinese will try to give some goods to everyone who attends the fair. If there is a shortage, prices rise regardless of world market conditions.

Pricing is another interesting aspect of dealing with China. The only actual cost of an item would be the imported content of the item. Other than this, you will find that capital-intensive goods tend to be far less competitive with the world market than those that have a high degree of labor content. Machines are a very valuable asset; time is less valuable.

There are no quantity discounts. You can spend a week negotiating a price on 100,000 units of a given item only to have another merchant from your country buy 5,000 units at the same price. The reason given: "We sell to all our Canadian friends at the same price."

One should be sure to buy and sell with caution. Trading with China is very different from trading with almost any other country. The people you send there will face unique problems and frustrations, and I would suggest that you give them broad discretionary powers within a particular frame of reference. Make every effort to have your people stay for as many years as possible.

15

A REPORT FROM THE
CANTON TRADE FAIR
by B. T. Rocca, Jr.

I was one of about 30 Americans who were invited to the Canton Fair in the spring of 1972. This was the first time that any American businessmen had been invited to Canton by the People's Republic. There were said to be 4,000 to 5,000 foreigners there. By far the largest contingent was Japanese, but the greatest interest centered on the Americans.

Equally significant to me was the fact that the Chinese very evidently wanted to make sure that our stay was productive and satis- factory to us. They gave us VIP treatment—particularly significant because the American forces had started bombing Haiphong and Hanoi.

Although the Canton Fair has been held for about 16 years, the most important fairs have been those of the last six years. We were told that the Chinese do about 50 percent of their entire foreign trade at these fairs. It was my impression, after eight days at the fair, that they probably do more than 50 percent of their export business there but substantially less than 50 percent of their buying.

The main purpose of the Canton Fair is to display Chinese wares and to give the Chinese a chance to sell as much as they can to foreign buyers. However, since the representatives of the seven state trading firms are all there, it is also an opportunity for foreigners to meet all of them at one time and in one place. The Chinese buyers are very courteous but will say, "Thank you very much, but come back next week." Thus the people who want to sell to China at the Canton Fair come early and stay late. They spend a lot of time on the eighth floor of the Tung Fang Hotel, where there is a small bar serving beer and wine.

A director (and former president) of Pacific Vegetable Oil Corporation, San Francisco.

Attendance at the Canton Fair is strictly by invitation. We were told that there were some 2,000 groups seeking admission from the United States alone. These were not only business groups but cultural groups, medical associations, and even hiking groups. The Sierra Club, for example, which had previously sponsored climbing expeditions in the Himalayas, asked me to find out how they could get into China to climb some of the mountains. But China has very limited facilities to handle foreigners; and I don't think that the small number of invitations in any way reflects unwillingness to be hospitable to more Americans. The Chinese have limited numbers of seats on their trains and their planes; and until they can get more facilities, they are not going to invite many people and then have them dissatisfied.

In traveling to the Canton Fair from Hong Kong, we couldn't get a seat on the train, even though we were there half an hour early and had first-class tickets. But when we got to the Chinese border and changed trains, we all had comfortable seats in an air-conditoned car. At the border you walk across the bridge, go through customs, are served an excellent meal, and then board the Chinese train. While in transit each passenger is given his hotel room assignment. Everything is very well organized and very well run by the China Travel Service.

It is clear that the Chinese are going to invite only those whom they think are important to China. I think most of the Americans who were invited to the Canton Fair, except for the representatives from the chambers of commerce, had a long history of doing business with China or had been working toward an improvement in the relationships between our two countries.

We were housed at the Tung Fang Hotel, where most of the foreigners stayed (with the exception of the Japanese, who had their own hotel). This was a tremendous advantage, because we had an opportunity to meet businessmen from every part of the world, to exchange views, and to see how different countries are reacting to the experience.

The Canton Fair is conducted in three buildings that are not as large as you might expect for a country the size of China. In each building there are displays of wares, and around the periphery there are small rooms where the negotiations are held. The negotiations are conducted by teams of Chinese that invariably include a translator, one or more representatives of the foreign trade corporation, and usually a representative of the manufacturing company. It was my experience that the appointments they arranged weren't very helpful because they usually were with someone pretty far down the ladder. We soon learned that some of these people didn't know the answers. Then you had to find out who their superiors were—and they don't give you calling cards. I understand that before the Cultural Revolution they did so, but now you often don't know with whom you are speaking, or where he stands in the hierarchy, until you have had several meetings with him.

For example, Mr. Wong is introduced as a "member of the team," but you don't know his rank in the team. Then you ask to see his superior and find out there is somebody higher. Then you ask that man to see his superior; and eventually, by the time you leave, you are talking to the presidents of some of the corporations and getting much better answers.

Toward the end of our stay, the Chinese were very anxious to debrief us. I had several interesting conversations with top-level people who wanted to know our impressions of the Canton Fair. I was told by other foreigners that this was quite unusual. On my last day I had an opportunity, along with three other Americans, to meet the top people at the fair. They wanted to know what we thought of their fair and what we thought could be done to promote and develop trade between the two countries. They listened very attentively, and it was clear to me that they genuinely wanted to develop trade and friendly relations with the United States.

Their main interest appeared to be a wish to implement the decision, enunciated by President Nixon and Chairman Mao, that both countries are going to make an effort to develop, or redevelop, friendly relations. I don't think, however, that we are going to have a great volume of business soon.

China wants to buy essential raw materials and technologically advanced products—things they can't produce themselves or don't produce in adequate quantities. Their purchases will be as large as they can pay for and will include agricultural commodities, steel scrap, and chemicals. A limiting factor will be what they can export to earn foreign exchange.

I was very favorably impressed with the variety and the quality of goods on display at the Canton Fair. I believe there will be a very large market in the United States for Chinese rugs and textiles, all kinds of artifacts, handicrafts, and light-industry products and furniture. They make beautiful furniture. I was able to go around with some of the buyers for the large department stores. They would have bought a lot more if more had been for sale. The problem is that the Chinese production of this type of goods is not adequate to meet all the demand from all over the world.

China raises the most pigs in the world, and therefore a lot of pigskin. The Chinese manufacture excellent and inexpensive leather articles of all sorts, including sporting goods and shoes. There should be a big market for these goods in the United States, but the Chinese are already selling as much as they can manufacture in the rest of the world. In one instance I overheard a buyer say, "I'd like ten dozen of those." "I'm sorry. We can't give them to you. We are all sold out. Come back in October." The buyer said, "That is ridiculous. I have been asked to come 10,000 miles and then am told to come back in October. When I come in October, you will say, 'come in April!'" Subsequently this particular buyer did talk to the president of the appropriate state trading corporation; and when he went back the next day, they had some goods to sell him—for the November-December shipment. The earliest delivery that could be had on rugs was for February-March 1973. Thus China has a problem of increasing its productive capacity. It was said that the Chinese had increased their 1971 production about 10 percent over that of 1970. However, the Europeans in Canton doubted that the production increase had been this much and told me they were still experiencing delays in delivery on many items.

One of the most serious criticisms that I passed on to my Chinese friends at the Canton Fair was that business must be conducted solely through the state trade corporations. It was not my experience that the representatives of the trade corporations are highly knowledgeable about the world market in the commodities in which they deal. Their ideas of the market price, and prevailing terms and conditions, were not always current. It may be that I was talking to the wrong people. For example, in the case of a particular commodity that I know is of very great importance—hybrid planting seed—the traders didn't even know what it was. They wouldn't admit that they had any interest in buying hybrid planting seed but merely said, "That is up to the minister of agriculture." I said, "Okay, what do I have to do to talk to the minister of agriculture?" "Never mind. We will talk to him, and let you know." This is a very serious impediment to the development of trade. I hope that this will be changed in time.

If the Chinese really want to develop foreign trade, it is important that they not try to do all of their business at the Canton Fair. We recommended that they invite foreign agronomists and technicians into their country at other times than during the fair. I think there is a good chance that they will change this policy. At least they indicated to me that they might do so.

We also had an opportunity to discuss a few philosophical questions with the Chinese. One has to be impressed with their sincerity. They really believe that they have accomplished a great deal; and I agree, particularly in terms of social improvements. They have eliminated drug abuse and violent crime. You have absolutely no fear of traveling the streets in Canton, and I suppose it would be the same elsewhere. You have no concern about leaving your hotel room unlocked. Not only do you not lose things through theft, you can't even give anything away. As an example of this, I tried to give my room boy an unused roll of toilet paper, a very scarce item in China, but he would not accept it. By the same token, tipping is forbidden.

117

Economically, I think the Chinese are going to be seriously handicapped by their system, because they don't provide any incentives for individuals. This lack was quite evident in the conduct of business at the Canton Fair. At 5:30 each afternoon the music starts and there is no more business for the day. You may be talking about a million-dollar piece of business. "Never mind, come back tomorrow". This kind of attitude won't accomplish an economic miracle.

PART

VI

**LEGAL ISSUES
IN CHINA TRADE**

16

U.S. EXPORT CONTROLS
AND THE CHINA TRADE
by Rauer H. Meyer

Any American who proposes to export to the People's Republic of China should be acquainted with U.S. export controls and how they relate to the China trade. There are a number of government agencies involved in the control of exports. The State Department, for example, deals with exports of munitions and the Atomic Energy Commission with nuclear-related items. The Office of Export Control in the Commerce Department handles the bulk of the commodities and technology that are exported. The legislative basis of the Commerce Department's control is the Export Administration Act of 1969, as amended, which grants the power and calls for the act to be used to control exports to achieve three policy objectives: to promote national security, to further foreign policy significantly, and to protect the domestic economy from the excessive drain of scarce materials and to reduce the serious inflationary impact of abnormal foreign demand.

The legal reach of Commerce Department controls is broad. Both direct exports from the United States and reexports of U.S. commodities from other countries are controlled. The use in friendly countries of U.S. parts and components that are incorporated into products destined for third countries is also controlled. Control is exercised over exports of U.S. technology; and in certain specified instances, exports of foreign-made goods that are the direct product of U.S. technology are controlled.

The Commerce Department has two basic licensing techniques or devices. First, there is the general license, under which goods may be exported freely from the United States if certain conditions

---

Director, Office of Export Control, Bureau of East-West Trade, U.S. Department of Commerce.

are met. That is, products may be exported to identified destinations without the necessity of the exporters coming to the Commerce Department for explicit permission. The bulk of all U.S. exports today move under a general license. Second, there is the validated license, which is a specific license issued after receipt from the proposed exporter of an application on a prescribed form. The application of controls is very selective in terms both of commodities and of destinations. A commodity control list spells out which commodities need a validated license for which destinations and which commodities may move freely without a validated license to various destinations. The criterion for national security control, that is, the basis for requiring a validated license, is essentially a judgment that a given commodity has the potential for contributing to the development of the military power of any given country to a degree that would be detrimental to U.S. national security.

For twenty years there was a virtual embargo on exports to the People's Republic. The Commerce Department has moved out of that stance in stages. First, it indicated publicly that it would approve, selectively, the use of U.S. parts and components in foreign-made items destined for China. Then it authorized reexports; and in June 1971, President Nixon announced a list of commodities that could move freely to China under general licenses. In 1972, the People's Republic was moved to the same country grouping as the Soviet Union and certain other East European countries. The meaning of the latter step was, in effect, that in terms of the published regulations, there was no essential difference between treatment accorded the People's Republic and the Soviet Union.

What are the criteria for issuing a license? Generally speaking, insofar as China and East Europe are concerned, controls are exercised on a transaction-by-transaction basis. An application form must be filed, setting forth the details of the transaction. Certain supporting documentation is required: a statement from the consignee as to his intended use of the material and an undertaking that, if he changes his intentions, he will inform the Commerce Department.

Once an application is duly filed, it is regarded from a number of standpoints. What is the inherent nature of the product? Is it militarily useful? What is the customary use pattern of the commodity in the country of destination? Does it incorporate advanced, extractable technology? Is the end-user civilian-oriented or military-oriented? What particular use does he propose to make of the commodity? With respect to information regarding the end-user and end-use, the Commerce Department relies not only on what the consignee or co-consignee says but also on other intelligence that enables some fairly concrete judgment to be formed as to whether there is a risk of the commodity's being diverted to military or other strategic uses.

If there is such a risk, how real is it? The risk of diversion to strategic use is then measured against the advantages of permitting the transaction to be consummated.

This end-user and end-use restriction presents the Commerce Department with a particular problem insofar as China is concerned. Over the years, the East Europeans have come to accept the need to supply this information. The Chinese, judging from some transactions, do not yet understand the importance attached to this aspect of controls.

Nevertheless, it has been possible to license certain conspicuous transactions because, from the negotiations or from the information that intelligence has supplied, adequate circumstantial evidence could be found that the commodities in question were going to be used for peaceful purposes: aircraft, aircraft engines, and satellite ground stations. Transactions in which the commodity involved can serve both peaceful and very significant military purposes present problems. If the Commerce Department is unable to acquire the kind of information that will permit it to make a fairly clear-cut judgment about the security risk inherent in approving the transactions, issuance of an export license is unlikely.

A difficult dimension of export control is the determination of what technology may be exported. This is of some importance in the case of China because of what is anticipated will be a fairly keen interest in acquiring advanced U.S. technology. The difficulty lies in the nature of the commodity. Technology that embodies a risk is hard to define, and it is even harder to say when it is being exported. The Commerce Department has defined export of technology to be not only its shipment abroad in physical form, such as in a blueprint or a prototype, but also the oral conveyance of the information to a foreign national, abroad or in the United States, with the knowledge that the foreign national is going to use the technology overseas.

On the administrative side, the statutory authority for controls obligates the Commerce Department to consult with other agencies of the government that may have an interest in exports. This is done very extensively on policy questions or specific proposed transactions involving policy questions. Formally, it is done through a structure of interagency committees, so that there is regular consultation with not only the Defense Department and State Department and the intelligence community but also with the Atomic Energy Commission and the National Aeronautical and Space Agency. By its very nature this is a time-consuming process and is resorted to only if informal consultation does not suffice.

The Commerce Department is obliged to pay due attention to what its advisers say. When a major agency of the government disagrees with a proposed course of action regarding a license or an export control policy, the matter is carried to higher levels. Depending

on the problem and its significance, it can get to the secretary of
commerce or even to the White House.

In addition to seeking advice and information from other U.S.
government agencies, the Commerce Department is obliged to consult
other COCOM members. (COCOM is an acronym for a coordinating
committee composed of the NATO countries, minus Iceland, plus
Japan, which have agreed to maintain controls on an agreed list of
strategic items.) When an item on this international control list is
proposed for export to a sensitive destination, as an exception to the
general embargo rule of COCOM, the government of the country pro-
posing to ship the goods must have the unanimous approval of all the
other COCOM members.

The control system that has been described here can be characterized as a thicket. It one wants to cut his way through, he must acquire
an understanding of the procedural rules and regulations. He should
also educate himself, with the Commerce Department's help, on the
policy objectives of the Export Administration Act. Changes in controls occur frequently. There have been, for example, a number of
announcements of decontrol actions. These will continue as the commodity control list is reviewed. There will be a continued concern
about export of high-technology items. The government's concern
with such items will coincide or conflict with China's interests in
high-technology items. High technology is not necessarily synonymous
with strategic significance, but there is a relatively high correlation.

The Commerce Department is likely to continue to handle matters
on a transaction-by-transaction basis, which means that it will continue to be interested in the proposed end-use of the commodity involved. This approach permits it to discriminate between strategic
and nonstrategic uses and to approve more transactions than could
otherwise be approved. The policy for China will essentially parallel
control policy for the Soviet Union. Controls and licensing actions
will continue to be related to what is conceived to be the contribution
that exports might make to the military potential of China. This contribution is, of course, evaluated in a rather broad context: in terms
of the international climate, of U.S. foreign policy, and of the U.S.
economic and commercial situation. The Commerce Department is
very conscious, for example, of the present balance-of-payments
difficulties of the United States. The fact that, organizationally, the
Office of Export Control is in the Department of Commerce and in
that part of the Department of Commerce known as the Bureau of
East-West Trade, whose main function is to promote exports with the
Communist countries, is no coincidence. The design was that the
controllers would moderate what otherwise might be tunnel vision.
This is not to say that national security is going to be sacrificed
for purely economic and commercial considerations; it does mean

that, when balanced against all these other considerations, the national security factor might in some cases be outweighed.

17

CHINA'S LEGAL SYSTEM
by Jerome A. Cohen

Prospects for trade with China, we have been told, are good to excellent; and I generally agree, though I am somewhat less sanguine than some. The first thing one has to concede is that the data on which judgments must be made are very fragile. As for China's contract and legal behavior generally, we are just in the beginning stage of experience; and it's been rather difficult in past years to get many businessmen to discuss their China experience frankly.

I remember trying to inquire, in 1963-64 in Hong Kong, about the experiences of British trading firms there. With the best of introductions, I went to one of the directors of Jardine Matheson, which has had a long experience with China. I couldn't get anywhere. The fellow kept looking at my card and holding it up to the light as though, if he held it up long enough, it would say in lemon juice "CIA," or perhaps the name of one of their competitors, or perhaps that I was working for the U.S. consulate in Hong Kong, trying to find out whether the company was violating the Trading with the Enemy Act.

A lot has happened since 1971, and I would like to provide some general information about the legal system, so that we can determine its relevance to any potential dealings one might have with China. In addition, I would like to convey some of my more enduring impressions gained in six weeks in China during the summer of 1972. Whether knowledge of the legal system is important for doing business with China is a question that the Chinese have had to face because they are constantly being asked about their legal system by businessmen who come to Peking. More basically, the Chinese are asking themselves whether they really need a legal system; whether they need one to show to foreigners, whatever the reality of Chinese life is;

Director of East Asian legal studies, Harvard University.

and whether a legal system is really important for their economic, social, and political development.

Economic matters, as Barry Richman has made clear, are very much in flux. But with respect to legal matters, as I said in an article in the Washington Post in the summer of 1972, the whole thing is open. The Chinese are rethinking legal questions as well as economic, social, scientific, research, and military questions.

In the course of my visit, a few of us had a very enjoyable dinner with Chou En-lai. Chou knows everything about you when you go there, for he is carefully briefed just before you meet. While there, he turned to me with a twinkle in his eye and said, "I understand you have written a number of books about our legal system." He smiled, and a number of us took that as implying, in effect, that I was making more of their legal system than there really is. That may well be.

But certainly when one goes to talk to the foreign trade officials at the China Council for Promotion of International Trade, one immediately encounters a strong self-consciousness about this lack of a legal system and a defensiveness about it that is startling. I got quite a long lecture. They really do have a legal system, I was told. It is just that foreigners are always looking for the wrong thing. They are looking for national legal codes, such as they have in Taiwan or in Japan or in many of the continental European countries. This, of course, was an ironic complaint insofar as Americans are concerned, because we don't use codes in the United States; we have many pieces of independent legislation.

It was instructive to learn from Howard Hawkins (see Chapter 18) that when references were made to arbitration clauses, it was arbitration in Stockholm under the rules and procedures of the Stockholm Arbitration Law and the law of the Stockholm Tribunal that was meant. The law of China was not at issue in this case because it is difficult to know what it is and the Chinese legal system has been through a number of stages.

One could find parallels here to the stages outlined by Barry Richman regarding economic development (see Chapter 8). From 1949 to 1952, there was a period of reconstruction in which the Communists were trying to get the government organized, to do away with the counterrevolutionaries, and to do away with the landlords. There was also some liquidation of people in the urban sector. There were mass campaigns, like the "five anti" and "three anti" movements (1951-52) that had kangaroo courts dispensing some very harsh sanctions. Some were financial penalties and some took the form of forced labor for long periods, but many individuals were physically liquidated. I don't think we should overlook this.

For ten years I was an advocate of trade and of the resumption of diplomatic relations with China. I think our government was too slow in this matter; but I don't think we should overlook the facts of life in our current euphoria because we are in danger, I think, of going to the other extreme.

The period 1949-52 was an unattractive period. By 1953, with the decision to launch the first Five Year Plan, a Soviet-style economy for development, the Chinese had to decide to have a legal system to go with it. Essentially they imported the Soviet model, which the Chinese, given their legal traditions, formed into a highly Westernized legal system in the continental European sense. All of a sudden in 1954 a constitution appeared. Codes were drafted and people's lawyers began practicing in colleges of advocates. This period saw the beginning of legal education and the appearance of the identifiable buds of a legal system. There was some backing and filling, including more campaigns against counterrevolutionaires; but by 1957 the Chinese legal system was moving very much in the direction of the Soviet model.

Then came de-Stalinization. In its wake the legal system had a very different fate in China than in the Soviet Union. In the latter, in 1957 and 1958, de-Stalinization led to much law reform from which there has been some retreat lately. But in China it led, in effect, to the abolition of the existing embryonic legal system. In other words, there was a kind of post-constitutional era from 1957 to 1966. The lawyers' colleges closed down. The role of the prosecutors began to shrivel up. The police really ran everything, not in a judicial sense but in an administrative kind of apparatus where the courts were simply the rubber stamp for imposing the most serious sanctions upon the people. It was a highly articulated system of sanctions that ranged from criticizing somebody informally to execution. There was a well-organized police administrative apparatus, and no legal codes were promulgated.

Then the Cultural Revolution came along and smashed this beautifully organized system. There really was chaos in the cities, though much less in the countryside. But this situation couldn't last very long, and by 1967 the military was called in. For a few years the military ruled China exclusively.

When one visits Peking and other cities, the signs still say "Military Public Security Station"; but the military is receding in respect to the application of the legal system. It doesn't play any role, as far as I could tell, with respect to international trade. Indeed, when Americans are around, the Chinese try to keep the military people in the background. When you visit Peking University, although the president is said to be a military man, you are received by the deputy president, Professor Chou Pai-ren, who used to be a professor at Cal-Tech and is a sort of Grover Whalen for visiting Americans. The Chinese try to soft-pedal the whole military apparatus and to focus on only one side of China. Thus, Americans who go to China tend to experience a paralysis of the critical faculties that makes them come back praising virtually everything seen there. But I don't think we should be taken in entirely; because underneath this picture of order, of progress, of dynamism, are a coercive apparatus and some unhappy people. After all, Chairman Mao himself has estimated that 5 percent of the population is basically hostile to his views—and 5 percent of 800 million people is a pretty large group of dissenters that has to be dealt with and processed, or at least kept out of the way of foreigners.

In China we are seeing a society in transition. Everything is up for grabs. My own impression of the current period is that the Chinese have returned to the kind of well-organized disciplinary system that we would call a legal system. It is a system, nevertheless, strikingly different from our own. Its courts play a very limited role. In conclusion, my impression is that China is now well started in the process of resuscitating the organizational structure that existed prior to the Cultural Revolution and that it is, in fact, returning in large measure to the pre-Cultural Revolution set of institutions.

VII
A CASE STUDY
OF U.S. ENTERPRISE
IN CHINA

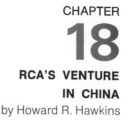

RCA'S VENTURE
IN CHINA
by Howard R. Hawkins

The development of trade with the People's Republic of China is an exciting and timely subject. Our new trade policy will be good for American business and for the peoples of the two countries. RCA Global Communications, Inc., a company that has communications operations with more than 80 countries, has business arrangements with both the China National Machinery Import and Export Corporation and the Telecommunications Administration of the People's Republic of China.

The Machinery Corporation is one of China's seven major foreign trade corporations and is responsible for the import and export of a wide range of machinery, electronics equipment, and technical know-how. The Telecommunications Administration is responsible for China's domestic and international communications services. It and RCA Glōbcom currently operate satellite communications circuits for telegraph, facsimile, and private-line services between China and the United States. Television transmission service via RCA also is available between the two countries. RCA Glōbcom is the only carrier providing that range of satellite communications services with China.

In February 1972, RCA Glōbcom installed the first transportable earth station at Shanghai under a contract signed on January 22 in Peking. That $2.9 million contract with the China Machinery Corporation, acting as procurement agency for the Telecommunications Administration, provided for sale of the earth station, microwave terminal equipment, and 20 units of a new video-voice system. The transaction marked the first major direct export sale from the United

---

RCA executive vice-president and chairman, RCA Global Communications, Inc. (Glōbcom), New York.

States to the People's Republic after President Nixon liberalized trade relations with that country. The Shanghai earth station was first operated to provide live television transmission to the United States during President Nixon's visit to China and also for telephone and telegraph services.

On August 17, 1972, in Peking, I signed two additional contracts for $5.7 million with the China Machinery Corporation. Li Chang Chin, deputy director general, represented the Machinery Corporation in execution of the contracts. They provide for the installation of a new earth station at Peking and for the expansion of the Shanghai station. The contracts contain options for additional equipment that could add another $.7 million in sales to China.

All three of the RCA Glōbcom contracts are cooperative arrangements with the Chinese Telecommunications Administration. Chinese civil and electronics engineers and technicians have undertaken the responsibility for earth station site preparation and building construction. They will work closely with RCA Glōbcom on antenna construction and electronic equipment installation. We will provide no more equipment and services than the Chinese want, and are happy to agree to such cooperative arrangements. They are consistent with China's posture of self-reliance and also are good business methods in trade with China.

The Peking earth station was completed by June 1973. It is used for direct satellite communications between Peking and other countries of Asia, Africa, and Europe. The Shanghai project was completed in August of 1973 for expanded satellite communications with the United States and other countries of the Pacific area.

The new earth stations are equipped with 98-foot-diameter antennas and advanced electronic equipment. They have highly efficient and cost-effective designs. Initially each earth station will be capable of simultaneous operation with four other stations and will have the capability for 60 voice-grade circuits plus television transmission. They can be readily expanded to much larger capacities.

These earth stations will provide China with the most modern international communications facilities for expanding the country's direct television, telephone, telex, and data communications links around the world. Indeed, the People's Republic will have made a great leap forward into modern international communications. The stations will operate with the high-capacity communications satellites in orbit over the Pacific Ocean that are owned by the 80-nation International Telecommunications Satellite Consortium rather than with Soviet communications satellites.

Trade with China does not come about automatically or by happenstance. The traditional hard sell or attempt at making a quick and sharp deal will not work there. To be invited to the People's

Republic, you must first establish your business purpose, credibility, and the need for your products or services. Understanding, know-how, and the correct approach are prerequisites for success. Never expect to fly in, make a fast sale, and leave quickly.

RCA Glōbcom's efforts at trade with the People's Republic began in July 1971, when we sent telegrams to the Peking Telecommunications Administration noting President Nixon's acceptance of the invitation to visit China. It was suggested that we jointly consider plans to re-establish direct communications services between our countries. We offered specific proposals for the improvement and expansion of those services.

The Shanghai Telecommunications Bureau replied on September 7 and agreed to restore the RCA radiotelegraph and radiophotograph circuits between San Francisco and Shanghai. That reply afforded the opportunity to begin anew direct communications with the People's Republic, broken nearly four years earlier. Radio operations were officially reopened in September.

We also made a series of further telegraphic proposals to establish an earth station in China not only for President Nixon's visit but also for continued satellite communications. We offered to send RCA Glōbcom officials to Peking for further discussions of specific proposals. In December an encouraging reply was received, including questions regarding sale of an earth station that were answered immediately. This was followed in late December by an invitation to visit Peking.

That opportunity called for a maximum response. We put together a top-flight RCA Glōbcom team for the January 1972 trip to Peking—three vice-presidents, all experienced in Far East negotiations and in satellite communications, and our Chinese-speaking satellite communications engineer. At the same time we intensified our preparatory efforts in New York for airlifting earth station facilities to China. Nobody had ever exported an earth station to China, and a license was required. Time was short, for President Nixon's visit to China was to take place in February 1972.

Following delicate, extensive, and at times uncertain negotiations in Peking, a $2.9 million contract for the Shanghai station was signed. That contract was short and without the detailed language customary in American agreements. Both sides were necessarily relying heavily on maximum cooperation and good faith to achieve the objective before President Nixon landed in China. Responsibilities and obligations of both parties were listed briefly. Thirty percent of the contract amount would be paid within five days. There were no escape clauses. The final paragraph (8) merely provided: "Any dispute arising during the execution of this contract will be settled through friendly consultation."

It was a momentous and unprecedented undertaking to assemble, transport, install, and check out the complex facilities within one month. Governmental and International Telecommunications Satellite Consortium approvals also were required.

We were restricted by the contract to sending only 20 engineers and technicians to China. Uniquely qualified RCA Glōbcom personnel were recruited from New York, San Francisco, Guam, the Philippines, Tangier, and Alaska. The earth station facilities were airlifted via Guam to Shanghai. That accomplishment no doubt impressed the Chinese and laid the foundation for the two subsequent sales to China by RCA Glōbcom. There is no substitute for friendly relationships and understanding coupled with performance in dealing with the People's Republic. At the same time, we could not have accomplished the objective without the cooperation of the Chinese engineers and technicians assigned to the Shanghai project. RCA Glōbcom technicians initially operated the Shanghai station while training the Chinese technicians. The latter quickly became qualified to operate the intricate electronic equipment, and they do so efficiently today.

Thereafter, we sent comprehensive technical and contract proposals to Peking for permanent installations at Peking and Shanghai. In April 1972, invitations were received to attend the Canton Trade Fair and thereafter to travel to Peking for discussion of our proposal. RCA Glōbcom executives spent the month of May in China negotiating with representatives of the China Machinery Corporation and Telecommunications Administration for the new Peking and Shanghai installations. This was by no means an easy undertaking, for the Chinese negotiators were skillful and dedicated. They knew what they wanted both technically and otherwise. Competing proposals also had been offered by several foreign and American earth station suppliers.

At the end of May, however, an agreement in principle was signed. A second RCA Glōbcom technical-legal team then spent five weeks of June and July in Peking finalizing details of the agreements. During the latter sessions the Chinese negotiators asked who would represent RCA Glōbcom at the contract signing in Peking. Upon being assured that an invitation would be accepted, the Machinery Corporation formally invited me, and my wife, to Peking to conclude and sign the contracts.

The Peking and Shanghai earth station contracts are fair and reasonable to both parties. They are comprehensive, each consisting of 20 pages of terms and several technical appendixes. Highlights include payment in U.S. dollars, an irrevocable letter of guarantee of performance executed by RCA Glōbcom, and an advance payment by the buyers of 30 percent of the contracted value. Any dispute in connection with the execution of the contracts shall be settled through "friendly negotiation." Failing settlement, arbitration shall take place in Stockholm, in accordance with the Swedish arbitration procedures and with reference to the Swedish arbitration laws.

Our experience in China trade indicates the following:

The Chinese are sincerely interested in developing trade with the United States, particularly with friendly Americans. It will be recalled that in the Sino-U.S. joint communiqué of February 28, both sides viewed bilateral trade as another area from which mutual benefit can be derived. They agreed that "economic relations based on equality and mutual benefit are in the interest of the peoples of the two countries."

In order to trade with China, you have to be invited; and you must first establish your credibility and business purpose. A detailed sales proposal should be sent in advance, so that the Chinese can consider it before entering into negotiations.

China's foreign trade corporations are the experts and represent the users. You should expect to deal with them while remaining cognizant of the ultimate users' needs and desires.

Negotiations should be friendly, cooperative, and flexible. Fair dealing and understanding are vital to success. Persistence and patience are required.

Contract negotiations were always conducted in Chinese and English through interpreters. However, all three of RCA Globcom's contracts were in English and only those documents were signed. Each page was initialed by representatives of both parties.

Keep in mind that the Chinese are excellent businessmen and that they have a different political system. The better you are informed about their country and their business methods, the more likely you are to be successful in China trade.

Top-level officials who have Far Eastern experience and who will approach the Chinese on a basis of equality and mutual trust should be your representatives in direct negotiations with China.

You may expect the Chinese to be considerate hosts if you are invited to China.

We were invited to China and went there as American businessmen for a specific purpose. Our hosts were always thoughtful and friendly, yet they were efficient and orderly in our business dealings. They seemed pleased with our interest in their country and exhibited a genuine interest in the American people. We were never subjected to any unfriendly action, though at times we attracted special attention from the Chinese crowds.

There were major differences between the environment of our original January dealings, when our negotiators were largely restricted to the Peking Hotel, and the relative freedom and reception of our August visit. I do not attribute the warmer atmosphere to what Pekingese call the "tiger heat" of August. Rather, it reflected the changes since President Nixon's visit and the Sino-U.S. joint communiqué of February 28 and, one hopes, the beginning of a new understanding between the peoples of both countries.

In conclusion, I should like to note that effective communications provide the means for supporting and stimulating international trade and foreign affairs. Modern communications are and should remain above ideological differences, as the means to transcend political, social, and cultural barriers that separate people and nations. To communicate effectively is the beginning of new understandings.

ACKNOWLEDGMENT

The statistical material which follows has been taken from People's Republic of China: An Economic Assessment, a compendium of papers submitted to the Joint Economic Committee, Congress of the United States (92nd Congress, 2nd Session), published May 18, 1972, by U.S. Government Printing Office, Washington, D.C.; also from People's Republic of China: International Trade Handbook, a research aid prepared by the Central Intelligence Agency, published October 1973, Washington, D.C. The material is reproduced here courtesy of the Joint Economic Committee and the Library of Congress—Ed.

CHART 1

China: Trade and Economic Trends

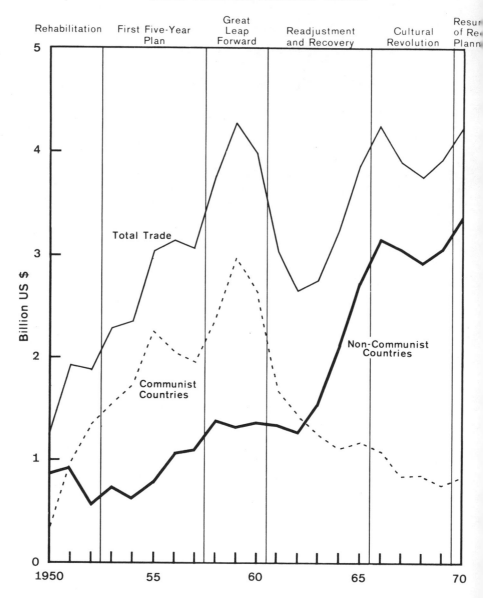

TABLE 1

China: Balance of Trade
($U.S. million)

Year	Total Trade				Communist Countries				Non-Communist Countries			
	Total	Exports	Imports	Balance	Total	Exports	Imports	Balance	Total	Exports	Imports	Balance
1950	1,210	620	590	30	350	210	140	70	860	410	450	-40
1951	1,900	780	1,120	-340	975	465	515	-50	920	315	605	-290
1952	1,890	875	1,015	-140	1,315	605	710	-105	575	270	305	-35
1953	2,295	1,040	1,255	-215	1,555	670	885	-215	740	370	370	0
1954	2,350	1,060	1,290	-230	1,735	765	970	-205	615	295	320	-25
1955	3,035	1,375	1,660	-285	2,250	950	1,300	-350	785	425	360	65
1956	3,120	1,635	1,485	150	2,055	1,045	1,010	35	1,065	590	475	115
1957	3,055	1,615	1,440	175	1,965	1,085	880	205	1,090	530	560	-30
1958	3,765	1,940	1,825	115	2,380	1,280	1,100	180	1,385	660	725	-65
1959	4,290	2,230	2,060	170	2,980	1,615	1,365	250	1,310	615	695	-80
1960	3,990	1,960	2,030	-70	2,620	1,335	1,285	50	1,370	625	745	-120
1961	3,020	1,530	1,495	35	1,685	965	715	250	1,335	560	775	-215
1962	2,675	1,525	1,150	375	1,410	915	490	425	1,265	605	660	-55
1963	2,770	1,570	1,200	370	1,250	820	430	390	1,525	755	770	-15
1964	3,220	1,750	1,470	280	1,100	710	390	320	2,120	1,040	1,080	-40
1965	3,880	2,035	1,845	190	1,165	650	515	135	2,715	1,385	1,330	55
1966	4,245	2,210	2,035	175	1,090	585	505	80	3,155	1,625	1,530	95
1967	3,895	1,945	1,950	-5	830	485	345	140	3,065	1,460	1,605	-145
1968	3,765	1,945	1,820	125	840	500	340	160	2,925	1,445	1,480	-35
1969	3,860	2,030	1,830	200	785	490	295	195	3,075	1,540	1,535	5
1970	4,290	2,050	2,240	-190	860	480	380	100	3,430	1,570	1,860	-290
1971	4,720	2,415	2,305	110	1,085	585	500	85	3,635	1,830	1,805	25
1972	5,830	3,055	2,775	280	1,270	750	520	230	4,560	2,305	2,255	50

Note: Rounded to the nearest $5 million.

141

TABLE 2

China: Trade by Area and Country[a]
($U.S. million)

Area and Country	1971				1972			
	Turnover	Exports	Imports	Balance	Turnover	Exports	Imports	Balance
Total All Countries	4,720	2,415	2,305	110	5,830	3,055	2,775	280
Non-Communist Countries	3,635	1,830	1,805	25	4,560	2,305	2,255	50
Developed Countries	2,240	810	1,430	-620	2,735	1,065	1,670	-605
East Asia and Pacific	1,005	365	640	-275	1,220	525	695	-170
Of which:								
Australia	71	42	29	13	105	55	50	5
Japan	929	322	607	-285	1,108	468	640	-172
Western Europe	985	410	575	-165	1,060	460	600	-140
Of which:								
France	192	67	125	-58	158	90	68	22
Italy	127	56	71	-15	162	74	88	-14
Netherlands	60	35	25	10	51	39	12	27
Sweden	56	16	40	-24	66	18	48	-30
Switzerland	42	23	19	4	39	17	22	-5
United Kingdom	161	69	92	-23	167	77	90	-13
West Germany	249	89	160	-71	282	92	190	-98
North America	250	35	215	-180	455	80	375	-295
Of which:								
Canada	241	28	213	-185	344	48	296	-248
United States	5	5	*	5	111	32	79	-47
Less Developed Countries	945	575	370	205	1,295	715	580	135
Southeast Asia	275	225	50	175	375	285	90	195
Of which:								
Indonesia[b,c]	35	30	5	25	40	35	5	30
Malaysia and Singapore[b,d]	185	150	35	115	205	160	45	115

142

Near East and South Asia	265	155	110	45	325	180	145	35
Of which:								
Egypt	46	15	31	-16	67	22	45	-23
Pakistan	63	31	32	-1	40	25	15	10
Sri Lanka (Ceylon)	58	26	32	-6	42	15	27	-12
Latin America	65	10	55	-45	240	25	215	-190
Africa	340	185	155	30	340	210	130	80
Other^e	*	*	*	*	15	15	*	15
Hong Kong and Macao	450	445	5	440	530	525	5	520
Of which:								
Hong Kong^f	431	428	3	425	513	509	4	505
Communist Countries	1,085	585	500	85	1,270	750	520	230
USSR^b	155	75	80	-5	255	135	120	15
Far East^g	225	150	75	75	260	180	80	100
Eastern Europe	445	195	250	-55	490	240	250	-10
Of which:								
Czechoslovakia	59	25	34	-9	55	30	25	5
East Germany	83	39	44	-5	94	47	47	0
Poland	58	21	37	-16	61	35	26	9
Romania	188	89	99	-10	216	102	114	-12
Other Communist Countries^h	260	165	95	70	265	195	70	125

*Negligible.

aData for individual countries, except where noted, are rounded to the nearest $1 million. All other data are rounded to the nearest $5 million.

bRounded to the nearest $5 million.

cOfficial statistics from Indonesia are believed to include re-exports of Chinese goods from Hong Kong and Singapore, as there have been no known direct imports of Chinese goods since 1966.

dAlmost all of China's exports to Malaysia probably are re-exported through Singapore and thus are double counted in the official statistics. To eliminate this double counting, estimates of China's exports to Malaysia and Singapore include only those imports reported by Singapore. The few exports that go directly to Malaysia are probably roughly compensated for in total trade to the area by re-exports through Singapore to Indonesia which have been reported as imports from China by both countries.

eIncludes Spain, Portugal, Greece, and Malta.

fNet of entrepot trade with third countries.

gIncludes North Korea, North Vietnam, and Mongolia.

hIncludes Yugoslavia, Cuba, and Albania.

143

TABLE 3

China: Trade by Area
(percent of total)

Area	1967	1968	1969	1970	1971	1972
Total	100	100	100	100	100	100
Non-Communist Countries	79	78	80	80	77	78
Developed Countries	50	50	50	52	47	47
East Asia and Pacific	21	19	22	24	21	21
Western Europe	26	25	24	24	21	18
North America	3	5	4	4	5	8
Less Developed Countries	20	19	21	19	20	22
Southeast Asia	8	8	9	6	6	6
Near East and South Asia	7	7	8	7	6	6
Latin America	*	*	*	*	1	4
Africa	4	4	4	5	7	6
Hong Kong and Macao	8	8	9	9	10	9
Communist Countries	21	22	20	20	23	22
USSR	3	2	1	1	3	4
Far East	6	6	5	4	5	4
Eastern Europe	6	7	7	8	9	8
Other	6	6	7	6	6	5

*Negligible.

TABLE 4

China: Major Trading Partners

Country	Total Trade 1972 ($U.S. million)	1972 Rank	1971 Rank
Japan	1,108	1	1
Hong Kong	513	2	2
Canada	344	3	4
West Germany	282	4	3
USSR	255	5	9
Romania	216	6	6
Malaysia/Singapore	205	7	7
United Kingdom	167	8	8
Italy	162	9	10
France	158	10	5

TABLE 5

China: Commodity Composition of Trade
(percent)

	1967	1968	1969	1970	1971	1972
Total Exports	100	100	100	100	100	100
Foodstuffs	26	28	30	31	31	31
Crude materials, fuels, and edible oils	23	21	22	21	20	20
Chemicals	4	4	4	5	5	5
Manufactures	44	44	40	42	44	43
Other	3	3	3	1	1	1
Total Imports	100	100	100	100	100	100
Foodstuffs	19	23	19	16	13	16
Crude materials, fuels, and edible oils	16	16	17	17	17	19
Chemicals	15	17	17	15	14	13
Manufactures	48	43	46	52	56	52
Other	1	1	1	*	*	1

*Negligible.

146

TABLE 6

China: Commodity Composition of Exports
($U.S. million)

	1971			1972		
	Total	Communist	Non-Communist	Total	Communist	Non-Communist
Total	2,415	585	1,830	3,055	750	2,305
Foodstuffs	740	140	600	950	200	750
Of which:						
Animals, meat, and fish	275	35	240	335	45	290
Grains	95	30	65	150	75	75
Fruits and vegetables	155	30	125	165	30	135
Crude materials, fuels, and edible oils	475	90	335	610	115	495
Of which:						
Oilseeds	15	0	15	15	0	15
Textile fibers	120	10	110	210	15	195
Crude animal materials	105	25	80	120	25	95
Chemicals	130	30	100	155	45	110
Manufactures	1,055	320	735	1,315	375	940
Of which:						
Textile yarn and fabric	325	80	245	440	115	325
Clothing	155	95	60	180	100	80
Iron and steel	65	25	40	60	25	35
Nonferrous metals	45	10	35	30	10	20
Other	15	5	10	25	15	10

Note: Data are rounded to the nearest $5 million. Estimates are based on data reported by trading partners. Where data are incomplete, as for most less developed countries and for many of the Communist countries, estimates are based on fragmentary information from trade agreements and press reports and on commodity breakdowns available for earlier years.

TABLE 7

China: Commodity Composition of Imports
($U.S. million)

	1971			1972		
	Total	Communist	Non-Communist	Total	Communist	Non-Communist
Total	2,305	500	1,805	2,775	520	2,255
Foodstuffs	290	70	220	450	30	420
Of which:						
Grains	205	0	205	345	0	345
Crude materials, fuels, and edible oils	385	75	310	520	80	440
Of which:						
Rubber	55	0	55	65	0	65
Textile fibers	140	0	140	195	0	195
Chemicals	325	20	305	355	25	330
Of which:						
Fertilizer	200	0	200	190	5	185
Manufactures	1,295	325	970	1,435	375	1,060
Of which:						
Textile yarn and fabric	40	0	40	40	0	40
Iron and steel	465	45	420	505	45	460
Nonferrous metals	150	10	140	225	10	215
Machinery and equipment	505	230	275	525	265	260
Other	10	10	*	15	10	5

*Negligible.

Note: Data are rounded to the nearest $5 million. Estimates are based on data reported by trading partners. Where data are incomplete, as for most less developed countries and for many of the Communist countries, estimates are based on fragmentary information from trade agreements and press reports and on commodity breakdowns available for earlier years.

TABLE 8

China: Commodity Composition of Trade with Non-Communist Countries, 1972

($U.S. million)

		Developed Countries[a]											Hong Kong and Macao[d]	Less Developed Countries[e]
	Total	Total[b]	Japan	Western Europe						United States	Canada	Australia		
				Total[c]	West Germany	United Kingdom	France	Italy						
Exports	2,305	1,065	468	460	92	77	90	74	32	48	55	525	715
Foodstuffs	750	255	117	125	43	13	20	14	4	6	2	300	195
Of which:													
Animals, meat, and fish	290	90	43	45	2	6	17	11	1	*	1	180	20
Grains	75	10	9	*	0	2	*	0	*	*	*	25	40
Fruits and vegetables	135	65	42	20	0	3	1	3	1	5	1	40	30
Crude materials, fuels, and edible oils	495	410	218	170	36	30	22	39	12	4	5	25	60
Of which:													
Oilseeds	15	5	1	*	0	*	*	*	*	0	*	4	5
Textile fibers	195	190	127	55	3	10	11	22	5	*	1	4	0
Crude animal materials	95	50	13	30	0	8	5	1	3	1	2	5	40
Chemicals	110	60	26	30	4	6	7	5	2	1	3	21	30
Manufactures	940	330	103	130	8	28	40	14	14	38	45	179	430
Of which:													
Textile yarn and fabric	325	140	45	45	1	11	14	6	3	15	27	50	135
Clothing	80	45	17	5	*	1	2	0	1	16	8	25	10
Iron and steel	35	*	*	*	*	*	*	0	0	0	*	12	25
Nonferrous metals	20	20	2	15	*	*	6	0	2	3	*	0	0
Other[f]	10	10	4	5	1	*	1	2	*	*	*	0	0

(continued)

TABLE 8 (continued)

		Developed Countries^a											Hong Kong and Macao^d	Less Developed Countries^e
				Western Europe					United States	Canada	Australia		
	Total	Total^b	Japan	Total^c	West Germany	United Kingdom	France	Italy					
Imports	2,255	1,670	640	600	190	90	68	88	79	296	50	5	580
Foodstuffs	420	340	*	*	*	*	*	0	75	262	5	0	80
Of which:													
Grain	345	335^g	*	0	0	0	0	0	75^g	261^g	0	0	10
Crude materials, fuels, and edible oils	440	120	23	55	7	8	2	4	2	12	25	0	320
Of which:													
Rubber	65	10	6	*	0	*	2	0	0	0	0	0	55
Textile fibers	195	50	16	15	5	7	0	4	0	0	13	0	145
Chemicals	330	310	209	100	45	6	5	22	0	1	*	0	20
Of which:													
Fertilizer	185^g	165^g	110^g	h	h	h	h	h	0	h	0	0	20
Manufactures	1,060	895	406	445	138	75	59	61	2	21	20	5	160
Of which:													
Textile yarn and fabric	40	40	32	10	0	4	5	0	0	0	0	0	0
Iron and steel	460	450	257	180	79	10	16	35	0	0	11	0	10
Nonferrous metals^i	215	75	10	35	1	13	5	0	0	21	9	0	140
Machinery and equipment	260	250	79	170	51	31	32	16	2	*	*	0	10
Other^f	5	5	2	*	*	*	*	1	0	0	*	0	0

*Negligible.

Figures are adjusted to reflect Chinese imports c.i.f. and Chinese exports f.o.b.

a Adjusted official figures except total Western Europe.

b Total of Japan, Western Europe, the United States, Canada, Australia, and New Zealand.

c Sum of adjusted official figures for Austria, Belgium-Luxembourg, Denmark, Finland, France, Ireland, Italy, Netherlands, Norway, Sweden, Switzerland, the United Kingdom, and West Germany.

d Exports are official data for Hong Kong plus estimates for Macao. Imports are estimates.

e Estimates based on very limited information. Complete commodity breakdowns are available for 1972 for only a small number of countries, and partial breakdowns are available for a few others. Estimates for the remainder are based on information for prior years and on information available on trade in particular commodities.

f Includes unreported trade.

g Freight adjustment was made independently, based on information on actual shipping costs.

h Complete information on fertilizer imports by country is not available.

i Includes official country data plus an estimate of nonferrous metals, especially copper, that are sold to China through the London Metals Exchange but have not been reported by the exporting country as sales to China.

Note: Figures rounded to nearest $5 million for total developed countries, total Western Europe, and less developed countries, and to the nearest $1 million for individual countries.

TABLE 9

China: Imports of Grain and Chemical Fertilizer
(millions)

Year	Grain		Chemical Fertilizer	
	Tons	$U.S.	Tons*	$U.S.
1966	5.6	400	2.5	155
1967	4.1	295	4.3	200
1968	4.4	305	4.0	200
1969	3.9	260	4.1	205
1970	4.6	280	4.3	230
1971	3.0	205	4.2	200
1972	4.8	345	4.0	190

*In product weight.

TABLE 10

China: Contracts for Whole Plant Imports, 1973

Nation/Firm	Type	Value ($U.S. million)	Contract Signed	Completion	Comment
Japan		306			
Toyo Engineering	Ethylene and butadiene	50	Feb 73	1978	Japan EX-IM/Commercial bank financing
Mitsubishi	Ethylene and poval	34	Feb 73	N.A.	Japan EX-IM/Commercial bank financing
Asahi Chemical	Acrylonitrile monomer	30	Mar 73	N.A.	Japan EX-IM/Commercial bank financing
Kuraray	Vinyl acetate and poval	26	Mar 73	1976	Japan EX-IM/Commercial bank financing
Toyo Engineering and Mitsui Toatsu	Urea and ammonia	42	Apr 73	N.A.	Japan EX-IM/Commercial bank financing
Toray and Mitsui Ship-building	Polyester chips	50	May 73	1976	Japan EX-IM/Commercial bank financing
Sumitomo	Benzene, toluene, and xylene	5	May 73	N.A.	Cash deal
Mitsubishi	Polyethylene, low pressure	22	Jul 73	1975	Japan EX-IM/Commercial bank financing
Sumitomo	Polyethylene, high pressure	47	Aug 73	1976	Japan EX-IM/Commercial bank financing
France		400			
Alsthom	Hydroelectric turbines (2)	10	Feb 73	N.A.	Consortium involving firms in France, West Germany, and the United Kingdom.
Speichem	Vinyl acetate and methanol	90	May 73	1976	
Technip and Speichem	Petrochemical complex	300	Sep 73	N.A.	French-led consortium probably involving other firms in Western Europe.
United States		75			
M. W. Kellog	Ammonia plants (3)	75	Mar 73	1976	Probable feedstock plants for the Dutch urea plants.
Netherlands		89			
Kellogg Continental	Urea plants (3)	34	Feb 73	1976	Subsidiary of M. W. Kellog
Kellogg Continental	Urea plants (5)	55	Sep 73	1977	Subsidiary of M. W. Kellog
West Germany		4			
Friedrich Uhde and Hoechst	Acetaldehyde	4	Jul 73	N.A.	
United Kingdom		8			
Technicolor Ltd.	Motion picture processing plant	8	Jul 73	N.A.	Cash deal
Total Value		882			

PAYMENTS

Most transactions in the China trade call for payment by irrevocable letter of credit (L/C) against presentation of sight draft and shipping documents. Letters of credit are negotiated on the Chinese side by the Bank of China (BOC), headquartered in Peking, with domestic branches in most ports of China. The three foreign branches of the BOC are located in Hong Kong, Singapore, and London. In negotiating letter of credit transactions, the BOC also utilizes an extensive network of correspondent banks established throughout the world in areas where China trades. For the United States, the BOC has arrangements with the branches of a number of foreign banks for negotiating letters of credit. As the normalization of U.S.-China relations continues, it is expected that the BOC will make similar arrangements with U.S.-controlled banks.

The L/C used in the China trade has a number of unusual features. The sales contract often specifies that the L/C provide for a margin above the original price to cover excess delivery charges or additional insurance requirements. When China is the seller, the standard form contract usually stresses that the buyer is to open the L/C promptly and may say little about the shipping and other documents which China is to present to obtain payment. When the PRC is purchasing, the documentation required by the BOC before it will make payment is spelled out in detail. It is also often stipulated that the L/C is to be opened with a BOC branch in China, in which case it is possible that the seller may be without goods or documents for a period of time. When the PRC is the purchaser, it may also refuse to follow the accepted international practice of having its letter of credit confirmed with a bank in the seller's country. However, the PRC has a well-established reputation for paying promptly and in full.

Until recently, the majority of contracts were negotiated in several West European currencies, including the British pound, the French franc, the Swiss franc, the West German mark and the Hong

---

From "Trading with the People's Republic of China," Overseas Business Reports, No. OBR 73-16, May 1973, prepared by John Phipps and JeNelle Matheson, Bureau of East-West Trade, U. S. Department of Commerce; courtesy of U.S. Department of Commerce.

Kong dollar. Now the Chinese increasingly insist on using the Chinese Renminbi ("People's currency", basic unit, the yuan) as the currency of payment. Renminbi has been the currency of payment in most recently reported contracts negotiated with U.S. firms. The PRC has concluded yen-yuan payments agreements with the major Japanese banks, under which Chinese and Japanese traders negotiate contracts in either the yen or the yuan, with balances periodically settled in third country currencies. The desire of the Chinese to increase the use of the yuan has been intensified by the successive devaluations and floatings of the principal world currencies.

Another recent trend of potentially great importance for U.S. firms is the apparent renewed willingness of the Chinese to seek and accept the use of medium term credit in its purchases. For the first time since the early 1960's PRC foreign trade organizations have concluded contracts for the purchase of complete plants with the payments deferred and spread over a period of up to 5 years at a 6% charge ("interest" is ideologically antithetical to the Chinese). Most of the transactions involving medium term credit have been with Japanese firms.

SHIPPING AND INSURANCE

Shipping for both exports and imports is handled by the Sinofracht Chartering and Shipbroking Corporation. Most export contracts signed by the FTC's specify that the buyer should not designate a particular shipping line or insurance company. While all seaports are officially open to foreign shipping, inland riverports are closed. American suppliers usually quote prices f.o.b. a major west coast port and c.i.f. Shanghai, where appropriate, although the Chinese now quote shipping c. & f. New York. At the present time, shipments are still made on third country vessels.

Shipment may be made from any Chinese port; the date of Bill of Lading is taken as the date of shipment. Any change of destination should be agreed to by sellers beforehand. Extra freight and/or insurance premiums thus incurred are to be borne by the buyers. In the case of f.o.b. shipments, if the cargo vessel fails to arrive at the loading port three days before the stipulated date, both the shipment and validity dates of the letter of credit will be automatically extended for 1 month, in which case the shipping agent's certificate must indicate the arrival date of the vessel.

For all shipments, including f.o.b., a late shipment penalty will be assessed for any late cargo and will be deducted from payments under the letter of credit. This penalty is usually 5% of the total value of the contract or part shipment called for in the contract, whichever seems justifiable to the buyer.

154

Insurance is usually handled by the People's Insurance Company of China. When the PRC is the seller, unless otherwise agreed, it will cover insurance at invoice plus 10% thereof of goods sold on c.i.f. basis. If the letter of credit stipulates transshipment of goods to an inland city or other ports, and/or insurance exceeds 110% of invoice value, the sellers will cover insurance on the buyer's behalf up to that city or port and/or to the percentage required, and the buyers are responsible for payment of the additional premium, which should be included in the letter of credit.

Claims for damage should be filed by buyers with sellers within 30 days after arrival of goods at destination and supported by sufficient evidence, otherwise the sellers may refuse to consider the claim. Claims that fall under the jurisdiction of the insurance company and/ or shipping company, are not considered by the sellers. Contracts usually stipulate that the sellers will not be responsible for late or non-delivery of goods when force majeure or other factors beyond the seller's control are involved.

In case of f.o.b. terms when the PRC is the buyer, the seller is responsible for: Sending to the buyer all information which he needs in order to book shipping space; any dead freight or demurrage which results from a delay in loading the shipment after the carrying vessel has arrived at the loading port in time; and all expenses and risks for the commodity before it passes over the vessel's rail and is released from the tackle.

The buyer or his agent is responsible for: Booking shipping space; furnishing sellers with enough information to arrange for ship- ment, notifying sellers of any change in carrying vessel or arrival date; and in the case of late arrival (within 30 days after arrival date) of the vessel at the port of loading, the buyer bears storage and insur- ance expenses incurred from the 31st day.

In case of c & f terms when the PRC is the buyer, the sellers are responsible for shipping the goods (without transhipment) from loading port to destination within the agreed shipment time and must then notify the buyers in order to arrange for insurance. In the case of parcel post/air freight, the sellers must furnish the buyers with sufficient information to enable them (buyers) to arrange insurance in time. Any losses incurred by the buyers because of seller's failure to cable in time to arrange insurance, will be borne by the seller. Any delays or non-deliveries due to force majeure will not be held against the seller if the buyers are notified immediately and furnished with a verified certificate of the accident. If there is more than a 10- week delay, the buyer can cancel the contract.

U.S. REGULATIONS GOVERNING TRADE
WITH THE PRC

Imports

With the exception of certain embargoed furs (ermine, fox, kolinsky, marten, mink, muskrat, and weasel furs and skins, dressed or undressed), goods may be imported into the United States from the People's Republic of China subject to the same general rules that apply to imports from other countries (i.e., proper labeling, food and drug regulations, etc.). Goods imported from the PRC, however, are dutiable at rates listed in column II of the Tariff Schedules of the United States. These rates are generally higher than those on goods from countries with which the United States has a reciprocal most-favored-nation (MFN) tariff agreement (Column 1 rates).

Information regarding the duties applicable to specific goods may be obtained by sending an adequately detailed description of the goods in question to the U.S. Bureau of Customs, 2100 K Street, N.W., Washington, D.C. 20226.

Exports

On February 24, 1972, the People's Republic of China was placed in country group Y for export control purposes by the Department of Commerce. As a result of this change, those goods exportable to the Soviet Union under general license, that is, without the explicit approval of the Department, may also be exported to the PRC under general license. The number of commodities requiring validated export licenses, that is, explicit approval, has been drastically reduced in 1973.

Firms wishing to export commodities or technical data to the PRC which may not be shipped under general license, may apply for a validated license from the Office of Export Control, DIBA-530, Department of Commerce, Washington, D.C. 20230 (Tel: 202-967-4293). It is recommended that firms requiring validated licenses consult with the Office of Export Control before attempting to sell these goods to China. While an official decision cannot be made except in relation to a formal application, the Department is prepared to offer informal advisory opinions that are helpful.

PRC TARIFFS

Imports by the PRC

Imported goods are assessed on the basis of c.i.f. including normal wholesale prices on support purchases, export duties, packaging costs, shipping charges, insurance premiums and a commission, decided by the customshouse after appropriate evaluation, for handling charges until the goods are unloaded at their destination. Imports, with the exception of bonded imports, must undergo customs clearance procedures or a customs duty must be paid within three months from the date a transportation organization reports the importation of the goods. If the procedures are not followed, the imported goods are subject to forfeiture.

Imports are classified into 17 groups, 89 types, and 939 items. There are two types of tariff rates for each commodity—minimum rates of 5 to 150%, applied to goods of those countries with which China has a reciprocal trade agreement, and regular rates of 7.5 to 400% for commodities of all other nations.

In general, construction materials, raw manufacturing materials and machinery are subject to lower tariff rates while higher ones are levied on silk fabrics, high-quality watches and cigarettes. Educational films and platinum are tax free.

However, for purposes of U.S. exporters, import licensing, customs formalities and tariffs do not exist as processes separate from the conclusion of contracts and need not concern the potential exporter.

Exports from the PRC

Exports are assessed on the basis of f.o.b. prices. All but 96 items, including peanuts, peanut oil, tung oil, peppermint and its oil, and pig hair are exempt from export duties.

TRADEMARKS, INVENTIONS AND COPYRIGHTS

China is not party to any multilateral or bilateral treaty with the U.S. relative to the protection of patents, trademarks and copyrights.

Trademarks

"Measures for the Control of Trade Marks," issued by the PRC April 10, 1963, and supplementary "Enforcement Rules," issued April 25, 1963, govern trademark protection in that country. Trademark applications are filed with the authorities in Peking, which handle their processing and examination, and issue certificates of registration. Marks registered by local enterprises have no fixed duration; they are valid until withdrawn by the registrant. Marks registered by foreign parties are valid for periods fixed by the registering authorities. The owner of a registered trademark acquires the exclusive right to its use in the PRC. Registered trademarks may be assigned.

A foreigner may apply for a trademark registration only if a reciprocal agreement exists between his country and the PRC. The mark must also be registered first in the applicant's home country. Since there is no reciprocal agreement on trademarks between the United States and PRC, U.S. parties presumably cannot register their marks in that country. Presently, the United Kingdom, Sweden, Switzerland, Denmark, Finland and Italy have reciprocal trademark registration agreements with the PRC. It may be possible, therefore, for a U.S. firm that has a subsidiary in any of these countries to assign its mark in that country to the subsidiary and then have the subsidiary apply for registration of the mark in its own name to the PRC. Foreign firms must contact the China Council for the Promotion of International Trade (CCPIT) to apply for trademark registrations in that country.

Other salient features of the PRC's "Trade Marks Measures and Rules" follow. The first applicant is entitled to registration; no prior use requirement is apparent. Not registrable are words or markings similar to China's national flag or other official emblems or medals, similar to national flags or emblems of other countries, similar to markings of the Red Cross or Red Crescent and "which have an ill effect politically." There are no opposition provisions, nor time limit for Governmental processing of applications. A trademark registration may be cancelled where the quality of the product does not meet Governmental requirements, where is is altered without Governmental authority, where the registration has not been used for one full year and no permission for such non-use has been granted, and where a third party applies for cancellation and, after examination of the reasons for this request by the Government, it approves the cancellation. For trademark registration purposes, there are 78 classes of goods. An application for a trademark for a medical product must be accompanied by a certificate approving the product's manufacture, issued by the Health Department. No foreign language may be used for trademarks, but trademarks with foreign languages may be used for export goods.

Inventions

The PRC has no patent law. All inventions and technology are considered to be State property. Indigenous inventions and technology are subject to the "Regulations on Awards for Inventions" and "Regulations on Awards for Technical Improvements," approved October 23, 1963, by the PRC State Council. These Regulations abrogated earlier Rules of 1950 and 1954 which had provided for some form of patent rights. The new "Regulations on Awards for Inventions" establish a system under which a party may apply to the State for official recognition of his invention. Should the State find his invention useful, the party is granted a registered certificate and given cash awards, and perhaps other bonuses based on the invention's use and value to the State, which retains ownership of it. Foreigners may apply for such registered inventor's certificates and be given awards on the same basis as those granted to PRC nationals. The new Regulations governing awards for technical improvements, as distinct from inventions, permit resident foreigners to submit such new technology to the Government and receive payments therefrom on the same basis as PRC nationals. There is no indication in the above cited "Regulations" whether payments to foreigners are remittable. The PRC reserves the right to sell to foreigners, through its Ministry of Foreign Trade, those inventions which are authorized for sale by the State Scientific Commission.

Copyrights

The PRC has not joined the Universal Copyright Convention or Berne Copyright Convention, or concluded any bilateral copyright protection agreement with the United States. So far as is known, U.S. authors have no copyright protection available in the PRC for their works first published outside that country. Thus, U.S.-authored books, plays, music and other literary and artistic works may be freely copied, translated and reproduced in the PRC without authorization from the copyright owner or compensation to him.

For further information on PRC's trademark and patent laws, communicate with the Foreign Business Practices Division, Office of International Finance & Investment, Bureau of International Commerce, Department of Commerce, Washington, D.C. 20230.

GOING TO THE PRC

Travel

The PRC may be reached by the following international air service: Air France, twice weekly to Shanghai; Pakistan International, twice weekly to Peking and Shanghai; Aeroflot once a week to Peking; Ethiopian Airlines, once a week to Shanghai. Other airlines will initiate air services to China in the near future.

Visas

Visa applications may be made in Hong Kong through either the Hong Kong or Kowloon offices of the China Travel Service (CTS).

Three copies of the visa form and four passport-sized photos are required. Normally, 4 days should be allowed between application for a visa and its receipt, although this may be changed to 5 days in the near future when new procedures go into effect. Visas may be picked up at the border station, Shumchun, at the CTS office in Hong Kong or at PRC embassies throughout the world.

In addition to the visa, an invitation of some form is usually required. Persons who have not received their visas prior to arrival in Hong Kong should produce evidence that their visit has the concurrence of an official organization in China. Without such evidence, an invitation from the appropriate Chinese authorities must be negotiated, a process which could take considerable time.

Health

For American travellers an International Vaccination Certificate bearing a current smallpox entry is necessary; however, if a traveller is coming from other areas where diseases such as cholera are endemic, other innoculations may be required.

Currency Regulations

The Chinese Travel Service in Hong Kong provides declaration forms for personal effects and the amounts of foreign currency to be taken into China. U.S. currency may be carried into China. The "declaration of foreign currencies" is held at customs until verified and is necessary for the exchange of traveller's checks or cash for Chinese currency. Foreign currency (including American dollars and traveller's checks) may be changed into Chinese Renminbi in the People's Bank of China located in the customs building at the border, and at appropriate locations within the country. Care should be exercised to keep receipts for money changed as an accounting is required at time of exit.

Prohibited Items

Personal items essential to the visitor during his trip and in reasonable quantity do not have to be declared and are exempt from customs duties and standard trade taxes. Limited amounts of clothing, foodstuffs, toys and local products as well as items for daily use and gifts not to exceed 50 yuan in total value are permissable after applicable standard trade taxes have been paid. Items exceeding the limits mentioned above may not be allowed in as personal effects.

Certain items are prohibited entry into China including Chinese national currency, lottery or raffle tickets, and any books, journals,

160

films, and tapes, which would be harmful to or cast aspersion on Chinese politics, culture and morals. Such items are subject to confiscation before entry.

VISITING IN THE PRC

Travel Facilities

For domestic air service, there are regular CAAC air services within the PRC. Trains are comfortable and efficient, although long distances may be involved. It takes 24 hours from Kwangchow (Canton) to Shanghai, and 30 hours from Kwangchow to Peking. Within the cities, taxis are available. Charges can vary from 25 to 40 cents per kilometer depending on the size of the taxi. There is a minimum charge for 2 kilometers. Since it is difficult to hail a taxi from the street, it is advisable to keep one's taxi for short shopping trips, or arrange with the hotel to be met by one following meetings.

Accommodations

Reservations can be made through the China Travel Service. The best hotels are the Hsin Chiao, the Peking Hotel and the Nationality Hotel in Peking; the Oriental Hotel and the Tung-Fang Hotel in Kwangchow. Most offer rooms with baths or showers and usually cost between $5 and $10 U.S. per night. Hotels normally offer inexpensive laundry services.

Restaurants

All hotels for foreigners offer both western and Chinese food. There are many fine restaurants in Peking including: The Large Peking Duck, The Small Peking Duck, The New Peking Duck, the Capital, the Minorities and a Mongolian restaurant in the Pai Hei Park. In Kwangchow: North Garden (Bei Yuan Fan Dien), South Garden (Nan Yuan Fan Dien), Friendship Restaurant (formerly Panchee) (You-yi Fan Dien), Moslem Restaurant (Hui-Min) and Floating Restaurant. When taking a party to a restaurant, meals may need to be ordered 12 to 24 hours in advance to allow for proper preparation.

Sightseeing and Entertainment

Inquiries may be made of the sponsoring trade corporation or the China Travel Service concerning visits to places of historical interest. Some of the more popular are:

Peking.—The Forbidden City, Temple of Heaven, the Summer Place, the Valley of the Ming Tombs and the Great Wall.

Kwangchow.—Tsung Hua Hot Springs.

There are frequent performances of the Chinese national opera, ballets, and theatre groups as well as sporting demonstrations. In addition, trips to nearby communes and factories can be arranged. Cars with drivers and guides may be hired through China Travel Service.

Generally, the initiative for entertainment should be left to the Chinese officials. Visiting businessmen normally find it difficult to reciprocate.

Social Customs

In China, the family name is always mentioned first, Thus, Mr. Teng Ho-ming should be addressed as Mr. Teng.

Normally a visitor will be invited to dinner at a restaurant during his stay, most often by the organization which is sponsoring his visit. Dinner usually begins about 6:30-7 p.m. The guest should arrive on time or a little early. The host normally toasts his guest at an early stage in the meal with the guest reciprocating after a short interval. The usual procedure is to leave shortly after the meal is finished. The guest makes the first move to depart.

Tipping is forbidden. However, it is appropriate to thank the hotel staff and other service people for their efforts on your behalf.

Generally, gifts should be utilitarian in nature and presented by informing the host agency that they have been left in the anteroom, that is, the gifts should not be directly presented. There should be one gift for each person. Technical and U.S. travel books make excellent gifts if free of propaganda or maps of China showing Taiwan or borders with the U.S.S.R.

It is customary to present business cards and helpful with one side printed in Chinese. Presentation of cards may not be reciprocated. Cards may easily be printed in Chinese in Hong Kong.

Visitors should conduct themselves with restraint and refrain from loud boisterous actions. Chinese social customs are conservative, particularly where pornography is involved.

Photography

Generally, photographs are allowed although the Chinese may exhibit sensitivity to shots of airports, bridges, ports and the like or anything of military significance. If there is a doubt as to the suitability of the subject, consult your tourist guide or a Chinese official before taking the picture.

Only certain brands of film can be processed in the PRC: Agfa Color and Sakura both positive and negative, Fuji Color only negative and Ektachrome only positive. Undeveloped film may be taken out of the PRC.

Dress

In Peking from December to March, it is very cold and visitors are advised to dress very warmly. In summer in north China and during the greater part of the year in the south, tropical or light-weight clothing may be worn. Visitors to the Kwangchow Fair dress informally in opennecked sport shirts and light-weight trousers. A light-weight pullover may be useful in the evening. It is also advisable to take cool, comfortable footwear and a light-weight hat.

Climate

In North China the temperature ranges from $5°$ F in January to $104°$ in July and August. Exceedingly dry and dusty for most of the year, Peking becomes rather humid during the rainy season of July and August. South China is subtropical and fairly hot until the end of October. Around Shanghai in East China the climate is very similar to South China with much higher rainfall than Peking. Spring and autumn are the best times to visit China, from the point of view of temperature. Dust storms can be expected in north China during April and May.

Language

Chinese (also called Mandarin, Gwo Yu, and Pu Tung Hwa—common speech) is the national language, although several other dialects are frequently used, especially Cantonese in the South. The written language is uniform. Businessmen will find that the people with whom they negotiate either speak English or will have interpreters available. The Chinese Travel Service can advise businessmen on reliable translation services.

While descriptive brochures can be printed by exporters in the simplified characters currently being promoted by the Chinese authorities, they may not be understood by other Chinese living outside China and, hence, may be useless in areas such as Southeast Asia and Hong Kong.

Time

Peking, Shanghai, Kwangchow, and Hong Kong are in the same time zone, 13 hours ahead of EST.

Public Holidays

Official public holidays are Jan. 1—New Year, May 1—Labor Day, Oct. 1, 2—National Days. The 3-day Spring Festival (Chinese New Year) occurs in January or February, varying from year to year.

Hours of Business

Government offices and corporations are open 8 a.m. to noon and and 2 to 6 p.m. Monday through Saturday (with minor variations during the cold and hot seasons). Sunday is treated as a holiday. Appointments are rarely made before 9 a.m. and it is not advisable to seek a Friday afternoon appointment. The Chinese prefer to negotiate in the morning rather than during the afternoon. Business discussions tend to last longer than in the West.
Shops are open from 9 a.m. to 7 p.m. everyday, including Sunday.

Currency

The currency of China is called Renminbi (RMB) or people's currency. Basic units:

Yuan (Y) = 100 fen (cents)
jiao   =   10 fen

Notes are issued in denominations of Y10, Y5, Y2, and Y1; and 5, 2 and 1 jiao. Coins are issued in denominations of 5, 2 and 1 fen. The exchange rate in April 1973 was: RMB 2.0066 = U.S. $1.

Weight and Measures

Most of the PRC's foreign trade is conducted in the metric system but domestic Chinese weights and measures should be understood:

1 Jin (catty) = 1.102 pounds
1 Dan (picul) = 0.0492 tons
1 mou   = 0.1647 acres

The domestic Chinese measuring system is limited to agricultural accounting and shopkeeping.

Typing

Typing services are not available on a commercial basis in Peking. Hence, any delegation should bring along a secretary and a supply of stationery and other materials.

Electricity

Both single phase, 220V AC, 50 cycle and 3-phase 380V AC, 50 cycle power is in use. Plugs are normally 2 or 3 pin flat (5 amp), but in hotel rooms there is usually one connection for a 2-pin round continental-type plug.

Communication Facilities

The Peking telephone system is automatic, direct calls can be made to all principal towns and cities. Calls to Hong Kong can be made from Shanghai and Kwangchow. It is possible to make calls to London, Moscow, New York, and Paris from China. Calls to the United States can be made from Kwangchow and Peking.

There is no telex communication between Kwangchow and Hong Kong, even during the Trade Fairs, although such service should be available by late 1974.

While there is no direct U.S.-China mail service, letters, post-cards and printed matter can be sent to China either by air or surface mail. Surface mail takes 6-8 weeks for delivery, airmail only 10-14 days. There is no registration or insurance service for letters.

Emergency Contact of Visitors

In the event it is necessary to contact a traveller in China on an emergency basis, it is best to notify the China Travel Service in Hong Kong or the U.S. Liaison Office in Peking.

Exit Procedures

Before leaving the country, the traveller should exchange Chinese Yuan for foreign currencies, since Chinese money may not be taken out of the PRC. The traveller should insure that he has obtained permission to take souvenirs out of China, and has made arrangements for any luggage to be shipped separately.

Before exit, the traveller's declarations of personal belongings will again be checked. Valuable items such as watches, cameras, pens, and radios registered at the customshouse at entry must be brought out again on the visitor's return trip. Items forbidden to be taken out of the PRC will be confiscated. These include:

Chinese national money; gold, platinum, silver and other precious metals such as personal ornaments (unless they had been declared at entry), any books, photos, tapes, or other media which pertain to Chinese national secrets;

items of artistic value pertaining to the Chinese Revolution, history or culture. Permission of the Chinese Cultural Agency is necessary in order to export any ancient artistic items or books.

After clearing customs, the visitor must walk from the Chinese side of the border to the Hong Kong side.

CHINESE FOREIGN TRADE CORPORATIONS AND THEIR AREAS OF REPONSIBILITY

China National Chemicals Import and Export Corp.
    chemicals, rubber, petroleum, fertilizers, and pharmaceuticals
Erh Li Kou, Hsi Chiao, Peking
Cable: "SINOCHEM" Peking

China National Native Produce and Animal Byproducts
    tea, coffee, tobacco, forest products, spices, furs,
    bristles, feathers, casings, hides, and leathers.
82, Tung An Men Street, Peking
Cable: "CHINATUHSU" Peking

China National Light Industrial Products Import and Export Corp.
    general merchandise, paper, toys, sporting goods,
    china, jewelry and precious stones
82, Tung An Men Street, Peking
Cable: "INDUSTRY" Peking

China National Textiles Import and Export Corp.
    textile yarn, fabrics, manmade and natural fibers,
    clothing and knitwear
82, Tung An Men Street, Peking
Cable: "CHINATEX" Peking

China National Cereals, Oils and Foodstuffs Import and Export Corp.
    meat, grain, fruits, vegetables, fish, sugar, beverages,
    and animal feed.
82, Tung An Men Street, Peking
Cable: "CEROILFOOD" Peking

China National Machinery Import and Export Corp.
  machinery, transport equipment, bearings, instruments,
  and spare parts
Erh Li Kou, Hsi Chiao, Peking
Cable: "MACHIMPEX" Peking

China National Metals and Minerals Import and Export Corp.
  ferrous and nonferrous metals, ores, minerals, coal,
  cement, and hardware
Erh Li Kou, Hsi Chiao, Peking
Cable: "MINMETALS" Peking

China National Technical Import Corporation
  complete plants and technology imports
Erh Li Kou, Hsi Chiao, Peking
Cable: "TECHIMPORT" Peking

SELECTED BIBLIOGRAPHY

For Taiwan and Mainland China

on Economics, Trade, and Investment

by Patrick M. Boarman

NOTE

The purpose of this bibliography is to provide businessmen in particular and concerned citizens in general with a handy, carefully pruned index of the best recent work covering economic developments in contemporary China.

A wide range of sources, including existing bibliographies, has been consulted in compiling this listing, from which many valuable works in other languages and unavailable in English translation had necessarily to be omitted. Scholarly reputation, rather than ideology, has been the guideline used in selecting authors. References from formally Communist sources have been so identified. Publications have been further segregated on the basis of whether they are concerned primarily with pre-Communist China and the Republic of China (Taiwan) or with the People's Republic of China (Mainland China). To lessen possible confusion arising from the similarity of the names of the two Chinas, the descriptive titles "Taiwan and pre-Communist China" and "Mainland China" have been used throughout.

As a new era opens in U.S.-China economic relations, it is hoped that this bibliography will prove helpful to those who wish to deepen their understanding of one of the most fateful issues of our time.

TAIWAN AND PRE-COMMUNIST CHINA

Books

Chang, John K. Industrial Development in Pre-Communist China—A Quantitative Analysis. Chicago: Aldine, 1969.

China External Trade Development Council. Exports of the Republic of China 1971-72. Taiwan: The Council, 1972.

International Trade Centre UNCTAD/GATT. China (Taiwan) as a Market for Manufactured Products from Developing Countries. Geneva: The Centre, 1970.

Jacoby, Neil H. U.S. Aid to Taiwan. New York: Praeger, 1967.

168

King, Frank H. H. A Concise Economic History of Modern China.
New York: Praeger, 1970.

National Economy, Republic of China. Taiwan: China Publishing
Company, 1965.

Remer, Charles F. Foreign Investments in China. New York: Fertig,
1968.

Shaw, Kinn W. Democracy and Finance in China. Columbia Series
in the Social Sciences, No. 282. Reprint of 1926 ed. New York:
AMS Press, 1970.

Sun Yat-Sen. International Development of China. Reprint of 1953 ed.
New York: Paragon, n.d.

Taiwan Board of Foreign Trade, Ministry of Economic Affairs.
Foreign Trade Handbook. Taiwan: Ministry of Economic
Affairs, 1971.

Taiwan Council for International Economic Cooperation and Development. Annual Report on Taiwan's Economy—1970. Taiwan:
The Council, 1971.

Taiwan Ministry of Economic Affairs. Industrialization in the Republic
of China. Taiwan: China Publishing Company, 1968.

Taiwan Research Institute of Agricultural Economics, College of
Agriculture. Long-Term Projections of Supply, Demand and
Trade for Selected Agricultural Products in Taiwan. Taiwan:
Taiwan National University, 1970.

Articles and Monographs

Ames, E., and Ames, M. "Taiwan's Development Typhoon." Nation
(March 20, 1972).

Balassa, Bela. "Industrialization Policies in Taiwan and Korea."
Weltwirtschaftliches Archiv (Hamburg), Heft 1 (1971). Reprinted
in Industry of Free China (Taipei), August 1971. Includes tables.

Barnett, R. W. "China and Taiwan: the Economic Issues." Foreign
Affairs (April 1972).

Cheng Kao-wu. "Decade of Promise: Economic Indicators Reach New Highs and Give Indication That Boom Condition Will Continue Through the 1970's." Free China Review (Taipei), February 1971.

Economic Progress of Free China, 1951-1958. International Cooperation Administration Mutual Security Mission to China, (Taipei), November 1958.

"Economic Situation of Taiwan in 1969." Industry of Free China (Taipei), September 1970.

"Establishing a Business in Taiwan." Overseas Business Reports, May 1967.

Fel, W. H. "Economic Development in Taiwan." Industry of Free China (Taipei), November 1970.

Focus on Taiwan. San Francisco: Bank of America, 1968.

Gerschenkron, Alexander. Economic Backwardness in Historical Perspective, A Book of Essays. Cambridge, Mass.: Harvard University Press, 1962. Chapter on China.

International Economic Survey—Taiwan. New York: Chemical Bank, 1966, 1969.

Investment Laws of the Republic of China. Industrial Development and Investment Center, (Taipei), 1961.

Labor Law and Practice in Taiwan (Formosa). Washington, D.C.: U.S. Government Printing Office, April 1964.

Negandhi, A. R. "Management Practices in Taiwan." MSU Business Topics, Michigan State University Graduate School of Business Administration, Autumn 1971.

Statute for Investment by Foreign Nationals, Promulgated on July 14, 1954: As Amended on December 14, 1959. Taipei: Industrial Development and Investment Center, March 1966.

Sun, Y. S. "Industrialization on Taiwan." Asian Outlook (Taipei), December 1970.

Taiwan Council for International Economic Cooperation. Economic Progress in the Republic of China. Taipei: Good Earth Press, Ltd., 1968.

"Taiwan Economic Statistics." Industry of Free China, September 1970. Includes tables and charts.

Taiwan's Agricultural Development. Foreign Agricultural Economic Report No. 39. Washington, D.C.: U.S. Department of Agriculture, Economic Research Service, April 1968.

Taiwan's Agricultural Growth During the 1970's. Washington, D.C.: U.S. Department of Agriculture, Foreign Economic Research Service, May 1971.

Taxes in Taiwan. Taipei: Industrial Development and Investment Center, October 1965.

U.S. Department of Commerce. "Taiwan—Sustained Upsurge Boosts Demand; U.S. Suppliers Should Benefit." Commerce Today, July 12, 1971.

Wang, H. K. "A Review of the Development of Foreign Trade During the Past Two Decades in the Republic of China." Bank of China Economic Review (Taipei), July/August 1970.

Additional References

Further bibliographical material on Taiwan will be found in the section "China" in Journal of Asian Studies for September 1969.

Berton, Peter, and Wu, Eugene. Contemporary China: A Research Guide. Palo Alto, Calif.: Hoover Institution, Stanford University, 1967. This work contains extensive bibliographies on both Taiwan and Mainland China.

Central Bank of China, Foreign Exchange Department. Export and Import Exchange Settlements. Taipei: Central Bank, 1970.

Taiwan Buyers' Guide 1970-71. Taipei: China Productivity Center, 1971.

Taiwan Guide. Taipei: Taiwan Visitors Association, 1968.

Taiwan Trade Directory 1969-70. Taipei: Importers and Exporters
Association of Taipei, 1969.

Taiwan Statistical Data Book. Taipei: Council for International Economic Cooperation and Development, annual.

Trade of China; Chinese Maritime Customs. Taipei: Taiwan Inspec-
torate General of Customs, annual.

Tsu, E. T. Business Directory of Taiwan. Taipei: April 1970.

Tsui, T. K. Industry of Free China. Taipei: annual.

Tapes

The following audio-taped interviews with China specialists
available from the National Committee on U.S.-China Relations, 777
UN Plaza, New York City (212-682-6848):

"Does the U.S. Have Moral Obligations to Taiwan?" An interview with
Mark Mancall, professor of history at Stanford University, about
the moral implications in America's relations with Taiwan and
the Republic of China government based there. Time: 27 minutes (1971).

"Is Taiwan an Obstacle to U.S.-China Relations?" Edward Friedman,
associate professor of political science at the University of
Wisconsin, presents his views on the status of Taiwan in U.S.-
China relations. Time: 21 minutes (1971).

"The Taiwan Factor in America's China Policy: A U.S. Government
View." An interview with Thomas P. Shoesmith, director,
Office of Republic of China Affairs, U.S. Department of State.
Time: 22 minutes, 4 seconds (1971).

MAINLAND CHINA
Non-Communist Sources

Books

Buchanan, Keith. The Transformation of the Chinese Earth. New
York: Praeger, 1970. An admittedly partisan description of
the Chinese model for economic development.

172

Chao, K. C. Agrarian Policies of Mainland China: A Documentary
Study (1949-1956). Cambridge, Mass: Harvard University
Press, 1957.

Chao, Kang. The Rate and Pattern of Industrial Growth in Communist
China. Ann Arbor: University of Michigan Press, 1965.

_____. Agricultural Production in Communist China, 1949-1965.
Madison: University of Wisconsin Press, 1971.

Chen Nai-ruenn; and Galenson, Walter. The Chinese Economy Under
Communism. Chicago: Aldine, 1969.

Cheng, C. Y. Economic Relations Between Peking and Moscow: 1949-
1963. New York: Praeger, 1964.

Cheng Yu-k'uei. Foreign Trade and Industrial Development of China,
A Historical and Integrated Analysis Through 1948. Washington,
D.C.: University Press of Washington, 1956.

Cohen, Jerome Alan, ed. The Dynamics of China's Foreign Relations.
East Asian Series. Cambridge, Mass.: Harvard University
Press, 1970.

Cohen, Jerome Alan; Dernberger, Robert F.; and Garson, John R.
China Trade Prospects and U.S. Policy. Edited by Alexander
Eckstein. New York: Praeger, 1971.

Dawson, Owen L. Communist China's Agriculture. New York:
Praeger, 1970.

Donnithorne, Audrey. China's Economic System. New York: Praeger,
1967.

Driscoll, George. Basic Data on the Economy of the People's Republic
of China. Washington, D.C.: U.S. Bureau of International Commerce, September 1972.

Eckstein, Alexander. The National Income of Communist China.
New York: Free Press of Glencoe, 1961.

_____. Communist China's Economic Growth and Foreign Trade.
New York: McGraw-Hill, 1968.

173

_____, ed. China Trade Prospects and U.S. Policy. New York: Praeger, 1971.

Galenson, Walter. Chinese Economy Under Communism. Chicago: Aldine, 1969.

Hirschman, A. O. The Strategy of Economic Development. New Haven: Yale University Press, 1958.

Hollister, W. W. China's Gross National Product and Social Accounts, 1950-1957. Glencoe, Ill.: Free Press, 1958.

Hou Chi-ming. Foreign Investment and Economic Development in China, 1840-1937. East Asian Series. Cambridge, Mass.: Harvard University Press, 1965.

Hsieh Chiao-min. Atlas of China. New York: McGraw-Hill, 1972.

Hughes, T. J., and Luard, D. E. T. The Economic Development of Communist China, 1949-1960. Second edition. London: Oxford University Press, 1961.

JETRO (Japan External Trade Organizatoin). How to Approach the China Market. English version of Japan-China Trade Handbook. Tokyo: Press International, Ltd., 1972.

Joint Economic Committee. Mainland China in the World Economy. Hearings, April 5, 10, 11, 12, 1967. Washington, D.C.: U.S. Government Printing Office, 1967.

_____. An Economic Profile of Mainland China. Two volumes. I: General Economic Setting, the Economic Sectors. II: Population and Manpower Resources, External Economic Relations; appendix. Washington, D.C.: U.S. Government Printing Office, 1967. Republished New York: Praeger, 1968.

King, Frank H. Concise Economic History of Modern China. New York: Praeger, 1969.

Li, C. M. The Statistical System of Communist China. Berkeley: University of California Press, 1962.

Miyashita, Tadao. The Currency and Financial System of Mainland China. Seattle: University of Washington Press, 1966.

Myrdal, Jan. Report from a Chinese Village. Translated from Swedish. New York: Pantheon, 1965.

Myrdal, Jan, and Kessle, Gun. China: The Revolution Continued. New York: Pantheon, 1971. A Chinese Village revisited eight years later, in 1970.

Needham, Joseph. Development of Iron and Steel Technology in China. West Orange, N.J.: Saifer, 1971.

People's Republic of China Atlas. Washington, D.C.: U.S. Government Printing Office, November 1971.

Perkins, Dwight H. Market Control and Planning in Communist China. Cambridge, Mass.: Harvard University Press, 1966.

Pisar, Samuel. Coexistence and Commerce. New York: McGraw-Hill, 1970.

Prybyla, Jan S. The Political Economy of Communist China. Scranton, Pa.: International Textbook Company, 1970.

Pryor, F. L. The Communist Foreign Trade System. Cambridge, Mass.: MIT Press, 1963.

Richman, Barry. Industrial Society in Communist China. New York: Random House, 1969.

Salisbury, Harrison E. To Peking and Beyond: A Report on the New Asia. New York: Quadrangle, 1973.

Scalapino, Robert A. The Communist Revolution in Asia: Tactics, Goals, and Achievements. Second edition. Englewood Cliffs, N.J.: Prentice-Hall, 1969.

_____. Elites in the People's Republic of China. Seattle: University of Washington Press, 1972.

Shabad, Theodore. China's Changing Map: National and Regional Development, 1949-1971. New York: Praeger, 1972.

Stahnke, Arthur A., ed. China's Trade with the West: A Political and Economic Analysis. New York: Praeger, 1972.

Tawney, Richard H. Land and Labor in China. Boston: Beacon Press, 1966.

U.S. Congress, Joint Economic Committee. People's Republic of China: An Economic Assesssment: A Compendium of Papers. 92nd Congress, 2nd session. Washington, D.C.: U.S. Government Printing Office, 1972.

U.S. Senate, Committee on Banking and Currency, Subcommittee on International Finance. East-West Trade. Hearings, June and July 1968. Three volumes. Washington, D.C.: U.S. Government Printing Office, 1968.

Walker, K. R. Planning in Chinese Agriculture, Socialization and the Private Sector, 1956-1962. London: Frank Cass and Company, Ltd., 1965.

Wheelwright, E. L., and McFarlane, Bruce. The Chinese Road to Socialism: Economics of the Cultural Revolution. New York, Monthly Review Press, 1970.

Willmott, W. E., ed. Economic Organization in Chinese Society. Stanford, Calif.: Stanford University Press, 1972.

Wu Yuan-li. The Economic Potential of Communist China. Menlo Park, Calif.: Stanford Research Institute, 1963.

_____. The Economy of Communist China. New York: Praeger, 1965.

_____. The Steel Indusrty in Communist China. New York: Praeger, 1965.

_____; Buck, J. L.; and Dawson, O. L. Food and Agriculture in Communist China. New York: Praeger, 1966.

_____; Wu, Grace; and Ling, H. C. The Spatial Economy of Communist China. New York, Praeger, 1965.

_____; Wu, Grace; Sheeks, Robert B.; and Lau, J. Y. The Organization and Support of Scientific Research and Development in Mainland China. New York: Praeger, 1970.

Yeh Kung-chia and Liu, T. C. The Economy of the Chinese Mainland: National Income and Economic Development, 1933-1956. Princeton: Princeton University Press, 1965.

Articles and Monographs

Trade with Red China: An Informative Introduction. Philadelphia: N. W. Ayer & Son, 1971.

Business International. "China Trade I—Drafting a Strategy for China Trade." *Business International* (New York), May 7, 1971.

_____. "China Trade II—Dealing with a Centralized Market." Ibid., May 14, 1971.

_____. "China Trade III—Establishing Contracts." Ibid., May 28, 1971.

_____. "China Trade IV—Results of the Canton Fair." Ibid., June 4, 1971.

Business International. *Measuring the Mainland China Market*. Management Monographs. New York: Business International Corp., 1970.

_____. *Selling the Mainland China Market*. Management Monographs. New York: Business International Corp., 1971.

"China." *Far Eastern Economic Review Year Book*. Hong Kong: Far Eastern Economic Review, December 15, 1966.

"China Trade: Approval by 'Cross Section' of Congress." *Congressional Quarterly*, Executive Branch, Department of State, June 18, 1971.

Close, Alexandra. "Picking up the Pieces." *Far Eastern Economic Review*, April 13, 1967.

Dernberger, Robert F. "International Trade of Communist China." *Three Essays on the International Economics of Communist China*. Edited by C. F. Remer. Ann Arbor: University of Michigan Press, 1959.

_____. "Economic Realities." *Contemporary China*. Edited by Ruth Adams. New York: Vintage Books, 1966.

_____. "China's Foreign Trade: The See-Saw Pattern." *Columbia Journal of World Business* 3, no. 6 (November-December 1968).

_____. "Foreign Trade, Innovation and Economic Growth in Communist China." China in Crisis. Edited by Tsou Tang and Ping-ti Ho. Chicago: University of Chicago Press, 1968.

_____. "Prices, the Exchange Rate, and Economic Efficiency: Communist China." International Trade and Central Planning. Edited by Alan Brown and Egon Neuberger. Berkeley: University of California Press, 1968.

_____. "Prospects for Trade Between China and the United States." China Trade Prospects and United States Policy. Edited by Alexander Eckstein. New York: Praeger, 1971.

"Despite Thaw—No Bonanza in U.S. China Trade." U.S. News & World Report, February 14, 1972.

Doing Business with the People's Republic of China. Honolulu: Hawaii International Services Agency, Department of Planning and Economic Development, 1972.

"Doing Business with Red China—Myth or Reality?" U.S. New & World Report, May 10, 1971.

Eckstein, Alexander. Communist China's Economic Aid to Other Countries. Intelligence Information Brief no. 375. Washington, D.C.: U.S. Department of State, February 20, 1961.

_____. The Communist Economic Offensive Through 1963. Researc Memorandum, RSB-43. Washington, D.C.: U.S. Department of State, June 18, 1964.

_____. "There's a Certain Sense of Mystery." U.S. News & World Report, May 10, 1971.

_____, and Deutsch, Karl W. "National Industrialization and the Declining Share of the International Economic Sector, 1890-1959." World Politics, January 1961.

Emerson, John Philip. "Employment in Mainland China: Problems and Prospects." U.S. Congress, Joint Economic Committee. An Economic Profile of Mainland China. Washington, D.C.: U.S. Government Printing Office, 1967.

Federal Reserve Bank of San Francisco. "The New China Trade" and "China and the Future." Monthly Review, January 1972.

Fun Chen-mae. "Paying the Peasant." Far Eastern Economic Review, November 3, 1966.

Goodstadt, L. F. "The Great Divide." Ibid., February 2, 1967.

_____. "China: Wages in Command." Ibid., August 6, 1970.

Hoadley, Walter E. "The Economics of East-West Trade." Pacific Business (San Francisco), September-October 1971.

Hoffman, Charles. "Work Incentives in Chinese Industry and Agriculture." U.S. Congress, Joint Economic Committee. An Economic Profile of Mainland China. Washington, D.C.: U.S. Government Printing Office, 1967.

How to Sell to China. London: Department of Trade and Industry, Export Services Division, 1970.

"Indicators of Market Size for 25 Asia/Pacific Countries." Business Asia, January 8, 1971.

Jones, Philip P., and Poleman, Thomas T. Communes and the Agricultural Crisis in Communist China. Food Research Institute Studies 1. Stanford, Calif.: Food Research Institute, February 1962.

Klatt, W. "China's New Leap Forward." Far Eastern Economic Review, July 21, 1966.

_____. "A Review of China's Economy in 1970." China Quarterly, July/September 1970.

Kovner, Milton. "Communist China's Foreign Aid to Less Developed Countries." U.S. Congress, Joint Economic Committee, An Economic Profile of Mainland China. Washington, D.C.: U.S. Government Printing Office, 1967.

Kunze, Bernd. "Trade Relations Between the U.S. and China." Intereconomics (Hamburg) no. 9 (1971).

Laughton, J. D. "China Market Merits a Fresh Look." Board of Trade Journal, October 14, 1970.

MacDougall, Colina. "China's Foreign Trade." Far Eastern Economic Review, January 27, 1966.

_____. "A Tour of Chinese Factories." China Mainland Review, June 1966.

McCobb, John B., Jr. "Foreign Trade Arbitration in the People's Republic of China." New York University Journal of International Law, Summer 1972.

McQuade. "China Shows Little Trade Potential." Advertising Age, November 15, 1971.

Mah, F. H. "The First Five-Year Plan and its International Aspects." International Economics of Communist China. Edited by C. F. Remer. Ann Arbor: University of Michigan Press, 1959.

_____. Communist China's Foreign Trade, Price Structure and Behavior, 1955-1959. RAND Research Memorandum 3852-RC. Santa Monica, Calif.: RAND Corporation, October 1963.

Mulker, L. J. "Primer on Red China's Finance and Trade." Bankers Magazine, Winter 1971-72.

Munthe-Kaas, Harald. "Roads and Rails in China." Far Eastern Economic Review, February 17, 1966.

Nihon Kogyo Shimbun. "What to Expect from Sales to China." Business Japan (Tokyo), September 1971.

_____. "World's Largest Untapped Market." Ibid.

Price, Robert L. "International Trade of Communist China, 1950-65." U.S. Congress, Joint Economic Committee. An Economic Profile of Mainland China. Washington, D.C.: U.S. Government Printing Office, 1967.

Prybyla, Jan S. "Communist China's Strategy of Economic Development: 1961-1966." Asian Survey, October 1966.

_____. "China's Economy: Experiments in Maoism." Current History, September 1970.

Ray, Dennis M. "The Future of the Maoist Model of Development." Asian Forum (Washington, D. C.), April/June 1970.

Remer, C. F. The Trade Agreements of Communist China. RAND P-2208. Santa Monica, Calif.: RAND Corporation, February 1, 1961.

Richman, Barry M. "Chinese vs. Indian Development." Phonotape no. 519. Santa Barabara, Calif.: Center for the Study of Democratic Institutions, 1972.

Roberts, J. C. "Wonderland of China Trade." Burroughs Clearing House, February 1972.

"Rocky Road to China Trade." Newsweek, March 13, 1972.

Scalapino, Robert A. "Sino-Soviet Competition in Africa." Foreign Affairs, July 1964.

Smith, Charles. "Mao's Team Volleys for Trade." Business Abroad (New York), June 1971.

Smith, Edward Ellis. The People's Republic of China. San Francisco: Crocker National Bank, August 1971.

Sun, Norman. "Prospects and Problems of Trade Between Japan and Mainland China." Symposium on Economic and Social Problems of the Far East: Proceedings of a Meeting Held in September 1961 as Part of the Golden Jubilee Congress of the University of Hong Kong: Edited by E. F. Szczepanik. Hong Kong: Hong Kong University Press, 1962.

"Trade Unions—and Lin Piao." China News Analysis (Hong Kong), September 2, 1966.

"Traders Pin Hopes on Nixon in Peking." Business Week, February 12, 1972.

Tretiak, Daniel. "China's Latin American Trade." Far Eastern Economic Review, July 25, 1963.

Tung, Robert. "The Sins of the Capitalists." Ibid., September 8, 1966.

Uchida, Genko. "Technology in China." Scientific American, November 1966.

U.S. Central Intelligence Agency. "Communist China's Balance of Payments, 1950-1965." U.S. Congress, Joint Economic Committee. An Economic Profile of Mainland China. Washington, D.C.: U.S. Government Printing Office, 1967.

U.S. Department of Commerce. Export Control Bulletin, nos. 46 and 47 (1971); no. 59 (1972). Available from field offices of the Department of Commerce.

_____. "Mainland China Trade Pattern in 1960's Points to Sales Possibilities." Commerce Today, May 3, 1971.

_____. "Procedures in Trading with Mainland Chinese Detailed." Ibid., June 14, 1971.

_____. "Trading with the People's Republic of China." Overseas Business Reports, August 1971.

Wilson, Dick. "China's Economic Prospects." Contemporary China. Edited by Ruth Adams. New York: Vintage Books, 1966.

Wolfstone, Daniel. "Sino-African Economics." Far Eastern Economic Review, February 13, 1964.

Wu Yuan-li. "Conceptual Difficulties in Measuring China's Industrial Output." China Quarterly, January-March 1964.

_____. "The Economic Realities." Diplomat, September 1966.

_____. "Planning, Management, and Economic Development in Communist China." U.S. Congress, Joint Economic Committee. An Economic Profile of Mainland China. Washington, D.C.: U.S. Government Office, 1967.

_____. "Food and Agriculture in Mainland China." Current History (Philadelphia), September 1971.

Yeh Kung-chia. "Soviet and Communist Chinese Industrialization Strategies." Soviet and Chinese Communism. Edited by D. W. Treadgold. Seattle: University of Washington Press, 1967.

_____. "Capital Formation." Economic Trends in Communist China. Edited by Alexander Eckstein, Walter Galenson, and T. C. Liu. Chicago: Aldine, 1968.

MAINLAND CHINA
Communist Sources

Politics

A Great Decade. Peking: Foreign Languages Press, 1959.

Chai, Winberg, ed. Essential Works of Chinese Communism. New
York: Pica Press, 1969.

Hawkins, John N., trans. Educational Theory in the People's Republic
of China: The Report of Ch'ien Chun-jui. Honolulu: University
of Hawaii Press, 1971.

Jacobs, Dan N., and Baerwals, Hans H., eds. Chinese Communism:
Selected Documents. New York: Harper & Row, 1963.

Li Fu-ch'un. Report on the First Five-Year Plan for Development of
the National Economy of the People's Republic of China in 1953-
57. Peking: Foreign Languages Press, 1955.

Mao Tse-tung. "Let a Hundred Flowers Bloom." Complete text of
"On the Correct Handling of Contradictions Among the People."
Notes and introduction by G. F. Hudson. The New Leader, sec.
2 (September 9, 1957).

_____. Selected Works of Mao Tse-tung. Four volumes. Peking:
Foreign Languages Press, 1961-65.

The Great Socialist Cultural Revolution in China. Six pamphlets.
Peking: Foreign Languages Press, 1966.

Trager, Frank N., ed. Mao: War or Peace? New York: American
Asian Education Exchange, 1970. A collection of official statements from Communist sources.

Economics

Chung, Feng. "An Economic Policy That Wins, A Survey of Policy of
Readjustment, Consolidation, Filling out, and Raising Standards."
Peking Review, March 13, 1964.

Li Shu-cheng. "New China's Achievements in Agricultural Production during the Past Three Years." New China's Economic Achievements, 1949-52. Peking: Foreign Languages Press, 1952.

"Shih-pan-yen Supply and Marketing Cooperative Maps Out a Preliminary Plan to Transform Itself into a University of Mao Tse-tung's Thought." Ta-kung Pao (Ta-kung News, Peking), August 27, 1966. Translated in U.S. Department of Commerce, Translations on Communist China. Washington, U.S. Government Printing Office, D.C.: 1966.

State Statistical Bureau. Ten Great Years, Statistics of the Economic and Cultural Achievements of the People's Republic of China. Peking: Foreign Languages Press, 1960.

Wang Hsiang-shu. "The Myth of Diminishing Returns." Peking Review, October 28, 1958. Note: Peking Review superseded People's China in March 1958.

Yun, Chen. "The Financial and Food Situation." New China's Economic Achievements, 1949-1952. Peking: Foreign Languages Press, 1952.

TAIWAN AND MAINLAND CHINA

Newspapers and Periodicals

The China Quarterly. London.

Current Background. American Consulate General, Hong Kong.

Economic Bulletin for Asia and the Far East. United Nations Economic Commission for Asia and the Far East, Bangkok.

Economic Review. Bank of China, Taipei. Bimonthly.

Far Eastern Economic Review. Hong Kong. Weekly articles on China.

Foreign Trade Quarterly. Board of Foreign Trade, Ministry of Economic Affairs, Taipei.

Hong Kong Trade Bulletin. Department of Commerce and Industry, Hong Kong.

Hong Kong Trade Statistics, Exports. Department of Commerce and
    Industry, Hong Kong.

Industry of Free China. Council for International Economic Coop-
    eration and Development, Taipei. Monthly.

Modern Asian Studies. Cambridge University Press, New York.
    Quarterly.

Republic of China Taiwan Financial Statistics Monthly. Taipei:
    Central Bank of China.

Survey of the China Mainland Press. American Consulate General,
    Hong Kong.

"Taiwan." Far Eastern Economic Review Yearbook. Hong Kong:
    Far Eastern Economic Review, Ltd., annual 1962-70.

Taiwan Financial Statistics Monthly. Central Bank of China, Economic
    Research Department, 1967-72.

ABOUT THE EDITOR

PATRICK M. BOARMAN was appointed director of research of the Center for International Business in January 1972, having previously served as professor of economics on the faculties of the University of Wisconsin, Long Island University, Bucknell University, and the University of Geneva (Switzerland). Other experience includes economic consultantships with the Office of the Secretary of the Treasury, the Federal Pay Board, the World Trade Institute (New York), General Electric Company, the American Telephone and Telegraph Company, and the U.S. House of Representatives.

Dr. Boarman is the author of numerous books and articles in the field of international economics and is the recipient of many awards in the United States and abroad for his scholarly contributions, including the Distinguished Service Cross of the Order of Merit of the Federal Republic of Germany. He holds undergraduate and graduate degrees from Fordham University and Columbia University and a Ph.D. in economics from the Graduate Institute of International Studies of the University of Geneva. Dr. Boarman is a fellow of the Royal Economic Society and a member of the American Economic Association, the International Economic Association, and the American Association for the Advancement of Science.

ABOUT THE CONTRIBUTORS

A. DOAK BARNETT is a senior fellow at the Brookings Institution, Washington, D.C., and is a highly respected consultant and adviser on U.S.-China relations. He has published numerous books and articles in his field; and his predictions concerning the evolution of Sino-American relations, including the new trade dialogue between the United States and China, have been uncannily accurate. Mr. Barnett was born in China and has been deeply involved in China affairs throughout his career. Prior to joining the Brookings Institution, he served as foreign correspondent in Asia, as consul in the U.S. consulate general in Hong Kong, and as consultant to the National Planning Association. In addition he has been a research fellow at the Council on Foreign Relations, a member of the staff of the Ford Foundation, and professor of government at Columbia University, where he headed the university's contemporary China studies program.

DAVID C. BUXBAUM is president of the May Lee Import-Export Corporation, New York. He attended the Spring 1972, Canton Trade Fair, where he signed 26 contracts for a total of $1 million worth of Chinese small goods. A China scholar who is fluent in the language, Mr. Buxbaum was one of the few Americans invited to conduct advanced negotiations in Peking after the Canton Trade Fair closed. He represented, in addition to his own company, a number of American corporations interested in trading with the People's Republic of China. Mr. Buxbaum is a former college professor and a lawyer. His wide range of interests in the field of China studies includes the practical aspects of transacting business with the Chinese and the applicable laws and customs of China.

PAT CLEVER is president of Canadian Manoir Industries, Ltd., Toronto. He came to Canada from his native Germany in 1953 and embarked upon a singularly successful business career. In 1968 he brought about the merger of Manoir with several other important companies, one of which was Katz International Ltd., exclusive agent for China National Arts and Crafts Import and Export Corporation for the sale of Chinese porcelain and earthenware in Canada. Mr. Clever has been involved in trade activities with mainland China over a period of many years and has traveled extensively throughout the country.

JEROME ALAN COHEN, director of East Asian legal studies at Harvard University, is recognized as an authority on the laws of the People's Republic of China. In May and June 1972, he visited the People's Republic at the invitation of the Scientific and Technical Association of China. Dr. Cohen has served as consultant on China and Asian affairs to many business and governmental groups, including the U.S. Senate Committee on Foreign Relations. He is author of a number of books about China, the most recent being China Trade Prospects and U.S. Policy (New York: Praeger, 1971). He is a successful lawyer and has served as law secretary to Chief Justice Earl Warren and to Justice Felix Frankfurter. Dr. Cohen is a graduate of Yale Law School.

ROBERT F. DERNBERGER is associate professor of economics, University of Michigan, and a member of the Executive Committee of the university's Center for Chinese Studies. Dr. Dernberger is the author of a number of publications dealing with the Chinese economy and is a member of the Joint Committee on Contemporary China, the Social Science Research Council.

KENNETH D. GOTT is managing director, Business International Asia/Pacific, Hong Kong. He was formerly editor of Business

187

International, New York. He was the director of Business International's round table conferences held in Japan in 1965 and 1971 and directed a similar round table in Australia in 1967. He is the former manager of the Pacific Merchandise Agency in Melbourne and holds the Distinguished Service Award of the American Asiatic Association.

MARSHALL GREEN, currently U.S. ambassador to Australia, was formerly assistant secretary of state for East Asian and Pacific Affairs. In the latter capacity he participated with President Nixon, Secretary of State William Rogers, and Dr. Henry Kissinger in formulating the joint U.S.-China communiqué issued at Shanghai in February 1972. Subsequently he visited many heads of state in the Far East to explain and promote the spirit of that communiqué. Ambassador Green has been a career diplomat in the U.S. Foreign Service since 1945, when he graduated from Yale University. His assignments have included posts as consul general in Hong Kong and as U.S. ambassador to Indonesia. Ambassador Green attended the National War College and holds the Meritorious Service Award and the Annual Career Service Award from the National Civil Service League.

HARNED PETTUS HOOSE, currently an attorney-at-law practicing in Los Angeles, has represented numerous American companies seeking trade and business with China and has negotiated both sales and purchases on behalf of his U.S. clients with Chinese trade and government leaders. He served as nongovernmental voluntary adviser and consultant to President Nixon and to the National Security Council in connection with the preparation for the journey to China. He is consulting professor of international business, Graduate School of Business Administration, University of Southern California, and an adviser to International Community College. Mr. Hoose was born and raised in China and was a resident there for over 20 years. He speaks Chinese fluently.

HOWARD R. HAWKINS was elected an executive vice-president of RCA on June 7, 1972, at which time he was also elected to the corporation's Board of Directors. As executive vice-president, he is responsible for RCA Global Communications, Inc., RCA Alaska Communications, Inc., Random House, Inc., and RCA Records.
Mr. Hawkins joined RCA Global Communications in 1946 as assistant general attorney. He became general attorney in 1949 and vice-president in 1951. He was elected executive vice-president and a director in 1964 and president on June 3, 1966. Currently he is chairman and chief executive officer of RCA Glōbcom.
A graduate of Indiana University in 1938 with a B.S. degree in business administration, he received the degree of Doctor of

Jurisprudence with distinction in 1941. He served with the Federal Bureau of Investigation from 1941 to 1946.

Mr. Hawkins is a member of the bar of the U.S. Supreme Court, the state of New York, and the Federal Communications Commission. He was president of the Armed Forces Communications and Electronics Association, New York chapter, from 1968 to 1970.

GRAHAM METSON is currently trade officer, Bureau of East Asian and Pacific Affairs, Department of State. At the Bureau, he has served since 1968 as economic officer for the People's Republic of China desk. Mr. Metson has had extensive experience in the Far East as a career foreign service officer, including assignments in Mandalay, Rangoon, Taipei, and Hong Kong. He is a graduate of the University of California at Berkeley and is fluent in Chinese.

RAUER H. MEYER is the director of the Office of Export Controls, Bureau of International Commerce, U.S. Department of Commerce. In that capacity he administers the U.S. laws and regulations governing exports to foreign countries. He has been instrumental in formulating the guidelines with respect to U.S. trade with the People's Republic of China and with the Soviet Union. His career in government began as economist with the Office of Price Administration in 1941. Later he joined the Board of Economic Warfare, where he served between 1942 and 1945 as a commodity industry analyst. Since World War II, Mr. Meyer has held increasingly responsible positions in the U.S. Department of Commerce, culminating in his present assignment. He holds an M.A. in international economics from the University of Chicago.

BARRY M. RICHMAN is professor of management and international business at the Graduate School of Management, University of California at Los Angeles. Recently he has served as dean of Faculty of Administrative Studies, York University, Toronto. Dr. Richman is a widely known China scholar and has acted as consultant on China affairs to business, educational, and governmental organizations in the United States, Canada, and other countries. His articles on industrial management and trade in China and in the Soviet Union have become practical handbooks for Western businessmen who are trying to understand and conduct business with those two countries. Dr. Richman has served as a consultant to a number of U.S. government agencies, including various Senate and House committees, the Agency for International Development, the State Department, and the White House. Dr. Richman holds advanced degrees in economics and business administration from Columbia University.

B. T. ROCCA, JR., was formerly president and chairman, and is currently a director, of the Pacific Vegetable Oil Corporation, San Francisco. He is also a director of Pacific Oil Seeds, Inc., Stockton Elevators, Pacific International Rice Mills, Inc., and the Federal Reserve Bank of San Francisco. He is a member of the Regional Export Council of San Francisco and is a director and member of the Executive Committee of the Pacific Commodities Exchange, Inc.

Mr. Rocca was one of a very few U.S. businessmen invited by China to the Canton Trade Fair of April-May 1972.

WILFORD WELCH is a senior staff member of the International Operations Group of Arthur D. Little, Inc. In his work at Little, Mr. Welch has specialized in the economics and politics of China and Asia. He has gained extensive experience in the area as a teacher, a diplomat, and a consultant. He is the author of several books and numerous papers and articles on Asian economics and the China trade.

Prior to joining Arthur D. Little, Mr. Welch held a number of posts in the U.S. Department of State, including that of special assistant for Asian economic affairs. He is a member of the National Committee on U.S.-China Relations and has studied the Chinese language at Yale, Hong Kong, and Taiwan. He was on the faculty of New Asia College, Hong Kong, from 1961 to 1963.

DAVID WILSON has been the editor, since 1968, of the China Quarterly, published by the Contemporary China Institute at London University. The China Quarterly is the premier scholarly journal covering modern China. Mr. Wilson was a member of the British Foreign Service between 1959 and 1968 and was stationed in Peking from 1963 to 1965. He has an international reputation as an authority on China affairs.

YUAN-LI WU is professor of economics, University of San Francisco, and is a consultant in the field of China affairs to the Hoover Institution on War, Revolution and Peace at Stanford University. Dr. Wu was educated in China and at the London School of Economics, from which he received his Ph.D., and is the author or coauthor of seven books and many articles on the economy of the People's Republic of China. He is a fellow of the Royal Economic Society and a member of the American Economic Association, the Mont Pelerin Society, and the Institute for Strategic Studies, London.

Dr. Wu served in the first Nixon administration as deputy assistant secretary of defense, international security affairs, Department of Defense.

ABOUT THE SPONSORS

The following persons have served as editors, sponsors, or organizers of the conferences on which this book is based.

TED R. BRANNEN became dean of the School of Business at the University of Southern California on January 1, 1972. He had previously been affiliated with the University of Houston, where his revision of the structure, programs, faculty, and curricula of the College of Business Administration had become a model of excellence for schools of business throughout the nation. Dr. Brannen has also served as administrator or faculty member at the University of Kansas City, the University of Florida, Texas A & M, and the University of Texas. He has been a consultant to leading industrial corporations, including Southwestern Bell Telephone, Continental, Humble, and Gulf Petroleum Companies, and the American Arabian Oil Company of Saudi Arabia. He has also served as economist and chief of the Economic Analysis Branch for the Southwest Region of the Office of Price Stabilization.

Dr. Brannen's Ph.D. is in economics and cultural anthropology from the University of Texas. He is the author of Overseas Management (New York: McGraw-Hill, 1965).

RICHARD C. KING is executive director of the Center for International Business. Previously he served as chief executive officer of the Birtcher Corporation, a major medical electronics firm with extensive overseas operations. Other experience includes three years as an independent management consultant, preceded by ten years with Kaiser Industries, with responsibility for corporate planning and, later, for government-relations activities in Washington, D.C., in the field of international affairs.

Mr. King's degrees are from Syracuse University and Occidental College. He is a member of the Los Angeles World Affairs Council and of the Defense Orientation Conference Association, and serves on the Advisory Council for the School of Agriculture of California's State Polytechnic College at Pomona.

JAYSON MUGAR, a native of Cyprus, is an international economics specialist at the Union Bank, Los Angeles. He has studied at Tufts University (Massachusetts) and at the Graduate School of Business Administration at the University of Southern California. He has also served in an administrative capacity at the latter institution. During a tour of duty with the U.S. Air Force in Hong Kong and Taiwan, Mr. Mugar gained practical experience in both Chinese business methods and the Chinese language, in which he is fluent. He has

191

served with distinction as a U.S. liaison officer to the Republic of China and has been the recipient of a number of awards and fellowships in international business.

DOYLE T. SWAIN was director of special projects at the Center for International Business during the period in which its China conference was held. He bore the primary organizational responsibility for the conference. His activities at the Center for International Business encompassed, in addition, political research, communications, and civic services. Mr. Swain served as administrative officer at Pepperdine University from 1960 to 1970 and at Harding College in the same capacity from 1950 to 1960. He holds a B.A. degree from Harding College.

CHINA AND THE GREAT POWERS: Relations
with the U. S. , the USSR, and Japan
edited by
Francis O. Wilcox

THE CHINA TRADE AND U. S. TARIFFS
Harry A. Cahill

CHINA'S TRADE WITH THE WEST: A Political
and Economic Analysis
edited by
Arthur A. Stahnke

DOING BUSINESS WITH CHINA: American Trade
Opportunities in the 1970s
edited by
William W. Whitson

EAST-WEST BUSINESS TRANSACTIONS
edited by
Robert Starr

SINO-AMERICAN DETENTE AND ITS POLICY
IMPLICATIONS
edited by
Gene T. Hsiao